THE ELEGANT
& EDIBLE GARDEN

THE ELEGANT & EDIBLE GARDEN

DESIGN A DREAM KITCHEN GARDEN TO FIT YOUR
PERSONALITY, DESIRES, AND LIFESTYLE

LINDA VATER

COOL
SPRINGS
PRESS

Brimming with creative inspiration, how-to projects, and useful information to enrich your everyday life, Quarto Knows is a favorite destination for those pursuing their interests and passions. Visit our site and dig deeper with our books into your area of interest: Quarto Creates, Quarto Cooks, Quarto Homes, Quarto Lives, Quarto Drives, Quarto Explores, Quarto Gifts, or Quarto Kids.

First Published in 2022 by Cool Springs Press, an imprint of The Quarto Group, 100 Cummings Center, Suite 265-D, Beverly, MA 01915, USA.
T (978) 282-9590 F (978) 283-2742 Quarto.com

Cool Springs Press titles are also available at discount for retail, wholesale, promotional, and bulk purchase. For details, contact the Special Sales Manager by email at specialsales@quarto.com or by mail at The Quarto Group, Attn: Special Sales Manager, 100 Cummings Center, Suite 265-D, Beverly, MA 01915, USA.

26 25 24 23 22   2 3 4 5

ISBN: 978-0-7603-7237-1

Digital edition published in 2022
eISBN: 978-0-7603-7238-8

Library of Congress Cataloging-in-Publication Data

Names: Vater, Linda, author.
Title: The elegant and edible garden : design a dream kitchen garden to fit
   your personality, desires, and lifestyle / Linda Vater.
Other titles: Design a dream kitchen garden to fit your personality,
   desires, and lifestyle
Description: Beverly, MA, USA : Cool Springs Press, 2022. | Includes index.
   | Summary: "With guidance from The Elegant and Edible Garden, you'll
   learn how to create a one-of-a-kind food garden that's just as beautiful
   as it is functional"-- Provided by publisher.
Identifiers: LCCN 2021043160 (print) | LCCN 2021043161 (ebook) | ISBN
   9780760372371 (board) | ISBN 9780760372388 (ebook)
Subjects: LCSH: Gardening. | Gardens--Designs and plans. | Kitchen gardens.
Classification: LCC SB473 .V38 2022 (print) | LCC SB473 (ebook) | DDC
   635--dc23
LC record available at https://lccn.loc.gov/2021043160
LC ebook record available at https://lccn.loc.gov/2021043161

Design and Page Layout: Rita Sowins / Sowins Design
Front Cover Image: Ryan Ford
Back Cover Images: Linda Vater (left), Ryan Ford (right) and Shutterstock (background texture)

Printed in China

I dedicate this book to all of my fellow gardeners
and followers around the world who are as passionate about
leading a garden-inspired life as I am.

CONTENTS

PREFACE

My garden passion started with a pumpkin *(Cucurbita)* seed. The seed was planted by a spent jack-o'-lantern from the previous autumn's Halloween. I was seven or eight years old, playing hide and seek, or maybe just exploring and adventuring, when I discovered the object of my new obsession—a massive, sticky vine with huge leaves growing on a thick, winding stem. It was hidden behind the foliage of a prickly Burford holly *(Ilex cornuta* 'Burfordii'*)* hedge next to the front porch of our suburban home in Tennessee.

I had no idea what it was, but it seemed wonderfully strange, otherworldly, and exotic. I would visit it several times a day throughout the summer to see what it was up to and check on its progress. At first, it was my secret. I kept it protected and hidden from my eight brothers and sisters. But eventually, the rampant grower escaped the bonds of earth and started to climb the hedge, eventually peeking out from behind the evergreen holly rectangle in search of more sun. I was mesmerized by how quickly it grew, the size of its leaves, and its mysterious presence. I had no idea what it was, where it came from, or what it would turn into. I just knew it wasn't like the other things growing around it, and it spoke to me. It befriended me. It had a vitality and personality and energy clearly different from other growing green plants in my young world.

The intrigue and distraction of that pumpkin vine also comforted me in a significant way. In the previous two years, I had lost my young, thirty-six-year-old mother and acquired a new one (then, soon after, I also had a set of new twin siblings). I also moved to a new state and was experiencing all the other raw and unfamiliar things that go along with those changes. But *this* new and strange thing demanded nothing of me emotionally, practically, or physically. This vigorous vine only required the gift of my attention and fascination, something I was ready, willing, and hungry to provide.

When the first yellow trumpet-shaped flower appeared, I was awestruck, and when the nubby flower base began to transform into a recognizable pumpkin form, my seduction was complete. It seemed like a miracle out of a storybook. Truth be told, it still does. Equally entertaining was figuring out how it had gotten there—playing detective and deciphering the clues that led to its identification—in that specific spot

The author, at home in her garden, watering the window box on her front porch.

Artichoke finials sit on posts leading into the potager to welcome visitors and adorn the entry.

A bee, a pollen-heavy flower, and a warm summer day—the essential DNA of a garden.

at that specific time. The sheer joy of waiting and watching and anticipating what would happen next kept me entertained all summer long.

Those months held other unexpected surprises: the incredible discovery of a large wild blackberry *(Rubus)* patch growing on an empty lot in the neighborhood and my first taste of sweet clover and nectar from a honeysuckle *(Lonicera)* flower. When I am stressed or anxious, I transport myself back to that field of those ripe, black, juicy berries—the warmth of the sun on my back, the tiny pricks from the thorny canes, and the taste of that perfectly ripe berry as opposed to the red underripe, bitter ones. I remember the delicious sleepy feeling of sitting in that field, hidden from view, my small frame warmed by the sun, blackberry seeds in my teeth, purple-stained fingers, and the delicious languor of a long summer day. In retrospect, it wasn't just the berries themselves, free for the picking. It was the *experience of them* that captivated my young self: their scent in the air, the play of sunlight on the field, the background melody of the lazy, humming, buzzing sounds of a living, breathing space and its inhabitants. And while I was in that field, I was a part

of it. I felt one with it. I sensed that I belonged there. It was my world as well as theirs.

As summer aged into fall and Halloween came around again, I had a newfound relationship to those pumpkins and seasonal gourds. They had shared their mystery with me, and I felt wiser and more worldly because of it. They were magnificent and fascinating to me in a different, more intimate way. We understood each other. We had fewer secrets between us. I now knew from whence those jack-o'-lanterns came.

That same fall, I learned that the bark of our sassafras trees in the front yard, with their distinctive fragrance and refreshing pungency, could be steeped to produce a cup of tea. I learned that those pumpkin seeds that produced a vine could also be roasted into a salty snack and that blackberries, if not consumed in one season— or in one picking—could be frozen for the next.

These were my first formative experiences with the concept of *growing my own food* (or more specifically in these examples, letting Mother Nature do it) and the inherent beauty of the process, from planting to harvest.

I sometimes have container garden parties in my small backyard. This one was specifically to create beautiful pot gardens for Mother's Day gifting.

Ultimately, and probably inevitably, I became a gardener, not just a forager. I learned to select and grow plants for myself and for my loved ones with happy intentionality: the plants I found most delicious, most beautiful, and most appropriate for my family and my life circumstances. As a gardener, I discovered that the *process* is as enjoyable and satisfying as the *product* of my labors and that beauty and elegance lie not just in the rewards, but also in the struggle of growth and creation itself. Most importantly, it became the center of a gardening way to live, and the sharing of all of it— the experience, the garden, and the harvest—with others. I invite you to share in this rewarding garden lifestyle right along with me.

INTRODUCTION

I have acute imposter syndrome writing this book. Why? Because I have no formal garden training, no degree in landscape architecture, garden design, or horticultural schooling of any sort. I am not even a Master Gardener. Maybe like me you have no garden design background, but also like me, you want to create your own dream garden and need the confidence and knowledge to start or expand one.

What little I now know, practically and aesthetically, comes from books, magazines, touring other gardens, and trial and error. What real-life education I have, I attribute to my gardening school of heartache and hard knocks. Nothing teaches quite like experience, the thrill of victory, and the agony of defeat—does it? I imagine many of you are in the same boat as I was—just trying to figure it out for yourselves: what comes first, how to progress, what to try, how to progress, and ultimately, ways to put your personal stamp on your garden. And while Mother Nature may be the supreme nurturer, she is also a tough disciplinarian who doesn't make learning easy. Nevertheless, I figured it out over time, and so can you. In this book, I want to flatten the learning curve for designing a beautiful, edible garden by sharing common-sense tips and inspiration and ideas from my own personal experience of starting a garden from scratch.

Even without great expertise, deep pockets, or a makeover television crew, you too can create a garden that appeals to all your senses—a garden that nurtures you, challenges your creativity, and feeds your appetite for joy, beauty, and healthy goodness in a practical, accessible way. How? Like I did—by just doing it. Start your own garden on whatever scale you can and with whatever resources you have. Create a garden that mixes the culinary delights of home-grown food with gorgeous, companionable ornamentals. You too can do all of this in an environment that suits you and your home. Think of it as the best kind of horticultural symbiosis, where the end results are far more spectacular to the eye, the palate, and your life than just the sum of the parts.

In late April, the cut flower bed in the potager is an orchestration of colors, forms, and textures.

Above: Picking fresh greens and herbs in the morning is a wonderful way to start the day.

Opposite: The inspiration for the arbor leading into my potager came from a similar one I had seen in my neighborhood. I took a picture of it so I could replicate it later.

In this book, I share how I, with little knowledge, skill, and resources, managed to create and design such a garden. And *yes*, as I am so often asked, I did 99 percent of the designing, digging, planting, and mistake-making along the way. I didn't do it all at once, of course. I started small, in scale and in budget, and with easy-to-tend plants that were often gifted to me by others. I learned as I went, enjoyed each small stage as I progressed, and then moved on to the next phase as I learned more. I ate the elephant that was and is my dream garden one bite at a time, absorbing as much as I could about gardening and garden design along the way. I became a sponge, soaking up bits and pieces of gardening information wherever I could and by paying attention to landscapes around me.

I discovered to my great delight that vegetables, fruits, berries, and nuts are inherently as beautiful as flowering shrubs, stately evergreens, and blooming annuals and perennials. Once I internalized this and liberated myself from the idea that vegetables go in one place in the landscape, and flowers, shrubs, and ornamentals go somewhere else, an amazing world of possibilities opened itself to me. Those tidy distinctive lines between edibles and ornamentals are blurring in contemporary gardens, and to magnificent effect. Marrying the aristocrats of the vegetable garden with the doyennes of flowering ornamentals against a backdrop of a strong garden framework—well, such is the thing of fairy tales.

Fabulous garden romances happen when you notice that the color of a stalk of chard *(Beta vulgaris* ssp. *cicla)* perfectly echoes the flower head of a tulip *(Tulipa)* or that red hot chili peppers *(Capsicum annuum)* planted with scarlet-colored salvia look fabulous as edging plants in the front yard border. Nature herself gives us all sorts of cues once we start paying attention and playing with her box of colors.

Plus, pinching a leaf of arugula *(Eruca vesicaria* ssp. *sativa)* or a nastrutium *(Tropaeolum)* bloom to taste its peppery zest is not only delicious, but it's also the essence of mindful living and appreciation of the moment. It's healthy, imminently satisfying, and, if grown responsibly, gives back to the earth

A storybook bunny feels right at home amidst cabbages, tulips, and pansies.

from which it was harvested. The season's first bite of a warm, freshly plucked cherry tomato is the taste of summer and the taste of success to new and experienced gardeners alike--and it's not difficult to grow.

These home-grown luxuries, fresh greens for your salad, fresh flowers for your table, and scented lavender for your bath are quite simply charming and engage our senses in ways that nothing else can. Going out into the cool of a morning, still in your nightgown, coffee or tea in hand, to check on the progress of the French breakfast radishes or the germination of a bean seed is a delightful, wonderful way to start a day—immediate gratification and daily motivation of the best kind. Before you know it, it becomes more than a garden. It becomes a way to live your life, to elevate the everyday and find joy and comfort in life's simple pleasures and the rhythms of nature. Even inevitable frustrations teach lessons. In the garden, there is always tomorrow and next year.

In the most difficult of growing seasons, I can take comfort in garden history. I feel one with other gardeners and our mutual struggles, both in the present and in the past. I can simultaneously channel my inner kindergartener and the frontier spirit of the earliest American pioneers by planting heirloom peas and nectar-rich flowers to attract pollinators. There is a rich legacy and community in gardening—in the sharing of knowledge and stories, as well as the harvest.

When we moved into this house thirty years ago, there was nothing in the front landscape but a very old oak tree in a "lawn" of hard-pan clay. The relatively small backyard contained exactly one aging eastern redbud *(Cercis canadensis)* tree, a nest of blackberry brambles, and an abandoned sandbox. Oh, and a huge clump of what I later identified as rhubarb *(Rheum rhabarbarum)*. *That* was the collective history of what this landscape was at that point in time. How's that for a place to start?

Over those thirty years, the gardens slowly grew, matured, and evolved—pleasingly enough to eventually be featured in numerous national magazines, in books, and on countless garden tours. It didn't happen overnight. I started my gardens at the same time I started my family, and neither happened easily. But they did happen *joyfully*—with toil, love, patience, and a good dose of humor and ibuprofen.

This isn't a book about soil pH, insect and fungal issues, or double-digging. Numerous resources containing far more valuable knowledge than I can share are readily available in multiple formats and online for free. This *is* a book about capturing the romance, the artistry, and the experiential nature of a garden and garden living. It *is* a book about designing a garden that is distinctly yours, using edibles as ornamentals, with lots of pictures for inspiration and emulation.

As a self-described garden evangelist, in this book and on all my other platforms, I want to share this message wherever and whenever I can:

If I did it, so can you.

To garden is to nurture--yourself, your family, your community, and Mother Earth.

PART I

ASPIRATION

"GARDENING SIMPLY DOES NOT ALLOW ONE TO BE MENTALLY OLD, BECAUSE TOO MANY HOPES AND DREAMS ARE YET TO BE REALIZED."

— ALLAN ARMITAGE

Chapter 1

BEAUTY AND SENSUAL APPEAL

DECIDE WHAT YOU WANT

When I began to write this book, I copied a bit of wisdom I'd read somewhere, and I put it front and center on my desk. It was a reminder to *"Don't think, just write."* Reading those words, it occured to me that what applies to writing very much applies to gardening. Research, reading, and observation are all well and good, but nothing advances a dream or a project quite like *doing it*—or more accurately, *starting it* somewhere. Anywhere. Just begin.

For you, starting your garden might be establishing a windowsill herb garden, installing a congregation of large pots on your back patio, or designing a full-blown kitchen garden on the back forty. To help you decide where to begin, it is helpful to know *what you truly want and dream of* within the personal constraints of what is possible. Constraints and limitations may be physical, financial, environmental—in other words, *reality-based*, yet manageable over time. *"What kind of garden do I really want?"* Asking yourself this important question will help you stay on track and focus on your end goal—despite these restrictions.

Also think about what jolts of inspiration you saw or read in garden books or in your gardening research that made your heart skip a beat? What magazine pages are dog-eared or garden books especially well-loved? What digital images are saved and visited like old friends, over and over again? Most importantly, *what do they all have in common?*

What homes do you drive or walk by regularly (usually ever so slowly) to see their landscapes, garden beds, and seasonal plant combinations?

Here's how this process worked for me. As I was beginning to create my own gardens, I defined a dream garden as anything resembling a design by Rosemary Verey, a legendary English garden designer, lecturer, and author. I came across an image of her famous knot garden in a magazine, and I immediately became obsessed with this image. I subsequently went down the proverbial rabbit hole on a hunt for more information about her gardens and how she developed her unique, personal garden style.

With her penchant for clipped boxwood *(Buxus)* and ornamental vegetable gardening, she soon became first and foremost in my heart and on my expanding garden bookshelf. Her books *Rosemary Verey's Making of a Garden*, *Rosemary Verey's Good Planting Plans*, and numerous others became constant companions of mine. These books captured the essence of her signature style—a strong, formal framework contrasted with the billowy abundant softness of blooming shrubs and flowers. She used edible and ornamental plants in a sophisticated way with great beauty and interest year-round. She divided her garden into multiple garden rooms with different visions and story lines for each one. Her approach captivated my imagination, envy, and attention.

Potager

French name for kitchen garden that combines vegetables and ornamental plants in beautiful designs. The origin is from the mid-seventeenth century, from the French words *jardin potager*—"garden that provides vegetables for the pot" or the soup (potage) pot. Literal translation would be "soup garden."

Above: The blowsiness of the flowers in bloom and the tightly clipped boxwood in Rosemary Verey's garden create beautiful tension between loose, blooming drifts and stronger architectural forms.

Left: As I designed my own potager, I kept in mind the wonderful contrast of clipped boxwood and loose, billowy forms to get the look I so admired in Rosemary Verey's garden.

Consequently, the exquisite details of my own garden daydreams began to take form after internalizing the book images of Verey's famous potager at Barnsley House. The images spoke of a way to live a domestic life with a beautiful garden at the heart of it, or, as Peter Mayle expresses it in his book *Encore Provence*, "The kitchen garden satisfies both requirements, a thing of beauty and a joy for dinner," requiting our appetites for both loveliness and deliciousness in many ways. I guess it was my first exposure to the concept of a *gardening lifestyle*, with the garden at the very heart of daily life, engaging all five senses both physically and spiritually.

As my personal gardening education continued, I began to understand through all that reading, gardening experimentation, and visiting local gardens and nurseries what I *didn't* want in a landscape and garden. Now I was trying to determine very precisely and very specifically what I *did* want and how to go about getting it. As importantly, and as a guiding influence, I wanted to know *why* I found the books about Barnsley House so appealing, and *how* I could translate this decidedly English gardening vernacular onto prairie soil in the United States, with a distinct Oklahoma twang.

A pilgrimage to the Cotswolds and Verey's famous home and garden at Barnsley House in Gloucestershire (which is now a high-end country resort and spa) was clearly in order. In the mid-'90s, I finally had the chance, and on a gray English afternoon, my husband and I were on her estate, alone wandering her gardens, snapping endless photos, and trying not to be overcome by the sheer enchantment of the place. I finally had a chance to demystify why her gardens so captured my own imagination.

When visiting other gardens for inspiration, let no detail go unnoticed. Note how the blue cushions of the furniture perfectly echo the color of the blue hydrangeas. Is this a technique you could employ in your own garden?

I think I needed to see her gardens through my own eyes to really decipher, in some way, what the magic formula was and how that formula might be applied to my own home and gardens with their inherent limitations—limitations that were geographical, financial, and, most importantly, spatial. Hers was a large country estate and mine was very small, decidedly under an acre in the heart of the city. Nevertheless, her gardens spoke to me, and I wanted to hear what they had to say, and, if possible, to apply that to my own aspirations for my garden world.

Above: Walking through an arbor of pleached apple trees at Barnsley House is all part of the magic and sensual appeal of this incredible garden.

Opposite A formal layout with strong lines and practical geometry softens with a touch of whimsy and personality. This charming scarecrow is up to the task!

From her prolific writings, I was very familiar with her different gardens within a garden: the famous Laburnum Walk, the Knot Garden, the Temple and Pool Garden, and the kitchen garden or potager. All were breathtaking of course, but it was her potager that grabbed me by the heartstrings and wouldn't let go. This was no simple, utilitarian vegetable garden. It was a world unto itself. It was an adventure. It was a sensory extravaganza of sight, sound, scent, touch and, yes, taste.

It was everything I felt a true kitchen garden should be, with storybook appeal, monastic calm, and common-sense planning. It was orderly, with patterns and textures and beautiful logic. It was a world where a person could lose themselves in mental, soulful, and physical ways. If imitation is the sincerest form of flattery, I wanted to flatter Mrs. Verey in whatever way I could.

Above: Fairy tales, and fairy tale gardens, indeed can come true. My own front garden was a sad and barren place when we bought this house, but it slowly became a landscape of beauty and delight.

Opposite: Brenton Roberts used surrounding features such as the stone building, a beautifully constructed wood pile, and a short stone fence to serve as a backdrop to his vegetable garden and express his inimitable style.

MAKE IT YOUR OWN

Inherent to the garden beauty of Rosemary Verey's garden was how well it fit into the surrounding landscape and complemented the style and architecture of Barnsley House itself. I have a 1932 Tudor home and consequently was drawn to gardens like Verey's that spoke the same language as my own aesthetic. For you, style cues might emanate from Thomas Jefferson's Monticello, the French Laundry Gardens in Yountville, California, or a l'orto Italian vegetable garden in Chianti. Or for the garden of your dreams, maybe it's a local community garden or a victory garden in the arid southwest United States.

I met someone recently who is creating her own chinampas, a floating garden crafted of woven materials, to create a giant floating raft on a shallow lakebed. These horticultural marvels were invented by the Aztecs to feed their growing population and are now finding renewed popularity around the world, even in the suburbs of Oklahoma City, apparently! Truly, inspiration is everywhere. Visiting gardens in other countries, environments, and planting zones is one of my favorite things to do when I travel. A gardener's hunger for new ideas to apply to one's own landscape is insatiable and not limited to just one style or type of gardening. Amazing and very different styles of gardening can be found the world over and are just waiting to be discovered through books, digital resources, and of course by touring the gardens themselves.

What all these aspirational gardens communicate to us is a sense of possibility and potential. The possibility that somehow what is so appealing and evocative about them can be translated into our own garden venues, no matter the scale or circumstances of how and where we cultivate our own patches of earth, even if it's just a congregation of pots on an apartment terrace. My own potager is nowhere as large and grand as Rosemary Verey's, but it *is* a modest version of what I was able to make possible within the confines of my own situation. If my own garden had been nothing but terracotta containers on my back porch, I nevertheless could

Above: Even the smallest of kitchen gardens can have an orchard. Consider planting dwarf varieties of your favorite fruit trees in good-looking large pots.

Opposite: Synchronizing the color palette of edibles such as cabbages *(Brassica oleracea)* with ornamentals like African lily *(Agapanthus africanus)* is one of the most enjoyable aspects of garden planning and planting. A true visual treat to the gardener and those who pass by.

have copied and applied many of the themes, plant selections, architectural shapes and forms, textural touches, and design notes from her unique garden.

So how exactly do we decode these gardens that we drool over in books, digital media, magazines, and real life? How do we unlock their secrets and find out what is possible for our own gardens and landscapes?

Start by being curious. Ask yourself questions that will help you deconstruct why you find a certain garden style, landscape design, or planting combination so compelling. Once you have some answers, try to translate what you love into what is possible in the context of your life, geography, and home.

Asking yourself questions helps you focus on the details of the design and specific garden elements. Many times, I have visited a garden I greatly admired but later simply remembered that

I liked it without details of particular features or atmospherics I could later re-create in some fashion in my own garden.

When you visit other gardens to help formulate your own garden goals, consider yourself a shopper. You are shopping for ideas: specific plant combinations, fence and gate styles, unique solutions to problems, and container garden possibilities. These are just some of the things that may end up in your shopping cart of gardening "AHA!"s. Total cost: nothing but your time and attention spent in the pleasant observation and analysis of a beautiful garden! It may be nothing more than seeing a series of stepping-stones laid in gravel, leading toward an outdoor faucet to prevent muddy feet, that proves just the solution you need to address that *same* problem in your own home garden.

When analyzing a garden, make sure to look up as well as down and across. Amazingly beautiful scenes may be unfolding directly above you. In my own garden, fall berries on Boston ivy (*Parthenocissus tricuspidata)* drip from a tree branch overhead.

Tip! Record Words that Describe a Garden's Appeal

For Barnsley House, I used rambling or walkable, orderly, variety, childlike, layered, levels, patterns, intimate, enclosed, awayness, crunchy, repetition, perfectly imperfect, contained, woven, pleasure, interplanted, colorful, entertaining, convivial, humming, quiet, calm, see through, fairy tale, fresh, country, and geometric. Then as you add to your garden, ask yourself if the elements you are adding contribute to the look that these words evoke.

In examining another charming garden on a local tour in my own neighborhood, I noted the use of creeping strawberries as an unexpected, beautiful, *and* edible ground cover. This popular red berry was used as an edging plant under a small allée of Japanese maples *(Acer palmatum),* crawling beside blue stone pavers in a side yard leading to the backyard and pool. I immediately recorded the idea. This whimsical and inexpensive solution is a perfect example of using an edible plant where an inedible ornamental ground cover would be the traditional selection. Their innovative use also proved particularly interesting to the youngest of the garden visitors who were surprised and delighted by their unexpected presence. I have copied versions of this idea many times for both beds and containers, in part sun or full sun, when a design called for a creeping or trailing ground cover. Even when hungry garden pests consume the fruit before the gardener

Eating berries picked straight from a garden path is a true joy and speaks to the child in all of us.

can harvest them, the frilly textured leaves and delicate runners remain handsome and do their job as a ground cover quite well, berries or no berries.

For many years, in my own garden, I had a wooden arbor at the entry to my potager and cutting garden. In the spring, it hosted one of the most fragrant cerise pink roses, a thornless climbing 'Zephirine Drouhin' rose (*Rosa* 'Zephirine Drouhin'), a beautiful variety I have recommended countless times. Every year in early spring, it would be covered on one side and over the top with a profusion of heavily scented blooms. But heat arrives early in my Oklahoma garden, sadly shortening the life of those magnificent deep pink flowers.

Happily, Mother Nature sometimes steps in later to fill the color void with volunteers of 'Red Pearl' cherry tomatoes (*Solanum lycopersicum* var. *cerasiforme* 'Red Pearl'). This very vigorous indeterminate grower serendipitously often goes to seed, overwinters, and germinates in the perfect spot to eventually scale the arbor. With a little training, this rambunctious grower proves a wonderful climber, with abundant clusters of beautiful red fruit adorning the arbor on the way up. One young visitor commented that the yellow flowers preceding the fruit looked just like a series of tiny Tweety birds resembling Snoopy's sidekick, Woodstock, clamoring up the vine. I will never look at a tomato flower waiting to be pollinated in the same way again. Neither will the mother of that very young garden tourist, I am willing to bet—someone who "shopped" this idea to bring home to her own.

THE MOST ELEGANT GARDEN IS A BEAUTIFUL AND HEALTHY GARDEN

Early in my gardening years, I was the classic novice gardener, acting and buying accordingly. My enthusiastic self would go to the nursery or garden center in early spring and be completely seduced by the expanses of happy, vibrant annuals in seemingly endless rows of flats in every color imaginable. At that point in my gardening education, color was what captured my attention, and, I thought then, was what defined what a beautiful garden was. Color and lots of it, in every shade and hue. I would naively select a few orange marigolds (*Tagetes*) here, a smattering of pink petunias (*Petunia x atkinsiana*) there, some colorful perennials, and maybe a few vegetables in six packs, then make my puny purchases and head home with optimism and high expectations.

In my fledgling new garden, I planted my pitiful darlings with no regard for soil preparation, light, or for each plant's individual requirements and preferences. If I had a bare spot in the garden bed with no weeds, I planted it. Inevitably, I soon had dead plants, no color, and only the sad remnants of crushed and empty plastic cell packs. I quickly learned that planting a flower or two as exterior beautification and design was a bit more involved and had a greater degree of commitment than putting a candlestick or frame on a fireplace mantle as interior design.

Dispirited, but still motivated, I began to read and learn about what plants, in general, need to thrive, and ultimately, what each plant specifically wants to make its contribution to an elegant and beautiful garden before adding it to the landscape. As a matter of fact, I continue to follow this dictum to this day. When I add a new shrub, vegetable, flower, or tree to my garden—whether new to me or new to the garden—I do current research as to what it needs and prefers to thrive. That said, like all true gardeners, I continue to make foolish purchases and have killed more than my share of any variety of plant. I consider it a cost of doing business as a serious gardener!

When I first started to garden, I researched information primarily from books and magazines, from gardening experts, and, to a certain extent, from the plant tag itself. These were not difficult to access resources and are, of course, still available to us today. Nevertheless, they are not nearly as easy or as plentiful as today's access to almost unlimited amounts of information online—with digital resources and horticultural knowledge literally at our fingertips in seconds. Ignorance of a plant's needs is now an unacceptable excuse when I kill yet another shrub or perennial. Now, if a plant in my garden fails to thrive because I didn't provide it the growing environment it needs, the cause, as they say, is usually operator error and laziness on my part, as I could have *easily* researched, then provided, what it needed to be healthy and happy at planting time. Now I try to use technology to identify plants and their needs, plant diseases, and problem pests whenever I can.

Opposite Above: A fragrant and thornless 'Zephirine Drouhin' rose climbs the arbor and intertwines with 'Climbing Old Blush' roses on the short fence leading into my potager.

Opposite Below: Learning what wants to grow in your garden is important, but so is knowing when to grow it. Pansies, violas, and chamomile if planted in the cool of spring or fall will flourish. Planting them too late as heat approaches will render them unhappy and very short lived.

Above: When I couldn't grow classic delphinium, the self-seeding larkspur (*Consolida*) proved an easier alternative, one that comes back reliably year after year and suits my garden well.

Opposite: It was a real epiphany to me (one I am embarrassed to acknowledge) when I realized a plant in a container that was no longer happy could be moved! These large variegated spiral boxwood (*Buxus*) topiaries were fine in spring but began to suffer dramatically in summer. Voila! I moved them into more shade, and they were happy and healthy again.

I say *easily*, but of course, that's not really true. Figuring out what a plant and a garden need is a balancing act, if not both science and art. How much water is just enough, and not too much? How much light is optimal—before it becomes destructive? How much fertilizer is necessary for more growth and blooms before we literally kill a plant with kindness and damage the environment in the process? Of course, if answers to these questions came easily, we would all be walking around with that proverbial green thumb. But the answers of course are nuanced and conditional; truly no one size fits all. Goldilocks had nothing on gardeners when it comes to getting things just right. So, when I get asked how often something in my garden should be watered or fertilized, I am compelled to give the most

unsatisfying of answers: "It all depends." The longer I garden, the more I realize that there are no absolutes or clear-cut formulas to follow, just generalities about a plant's needs that one must consider in the context of one's own growing situation.

For example, *full sun* is not the same in my Oklahoma garden as it is in a garden much farther north. For that matter, full sun in my own garden in the spring is not at all equivalent to full sun in a devilishly hot and dry late summer. So, research what a plant needs and wants in general, but consider the context in which *you* are gardening to help ensure its success in your own garden's environment. Keen observation of what is happy in others' gardens in your area will give you helpful clues as to what might be successfully grown on your own and in an

The moods of the garden, just like the moods of the gardener, change with the weather, the season, the time of day, and the quality of light.

environment similar to yours. Likewise, plants that are *not* grown in your locale will also give you an idea as to what might struggle there.

After trying unsuccessfully to grow perennial delphiniums *(Delphinium elatum)* year after year, I finally realized that there simply was not a good garden "fit" between that blue beauty and where and how I garden. I had seldom, if ever, seen a beautiful stand of them on my countless garden visits in my own growing zone, much less a seasonal display that came back reliably year after year. That should

have been my first hint, or the second or third, at the very least. Playing Nancy Drew by calling my local horticultural extension center and reading up on what conditions delphinium preferred would have been next on the list.

So, what to do when your eye, heart, and soul crave a certain plant, or the *look and vibe* of a certain plant, yet it doesn't want to participate in your horticultural romance? You are willing to make a commitment to it, but it doesn't want to make a commitment to you. Over the years and as someone who gardens in a notoriously difficult place, I have come up with these options. Consider it some free counseling. Plant-Gardener relationship advice, if you will.

1. *Simply don't grow it* and call off the relationship. Don't torture yourself and waste money and resources. Grow something that really wants to live where you garden.

2. Try to *identify a doppelganger* with a similar look, but that is adapted and amenable to your zone—a.k.a., move on to your next romance. For example, what I coveted, and thought of as the "classic" delphinium, is perennial and more commonly found in cold and wet climates and at higher altitudes. Larkspur (*Consolida*) proved a much better fit to my Oklahoma garden.

3. But what if you simply can't deny yourself that flower/fruit tree/herb? You tell me your very soul insists you cultivate it? Your love remains unrequited. Then grow it! But you must be prepared to suffer and/or be disappointed and dissatisfied far more often than rewarded by its presence in your garden.

For example, I *adore* foxglove (*Digitalis)* and try to grow it every year. Try being the operative word. My gardening vanity and English garden illusions demand it. Where you live, it may grow almost like a weed, self-seed reliably, and appear seemingly by magic each season. Not so in my heavy red clay soil with high, desiccating winds; extreme heat; and rampant summer spider mite population. Still, I persist in my folly year after year. Most years it does so-so. Some years it's an almost no-show. But those few years when it is simply lovely, whimsical, and a pollinator extraordinaire—well, it is for that intermittent reinforcement that I risk disappointment on an annual basis. It may be an unhealthy relationship, but I go into it wide-eyed and realistic from the get-go.

I have learned some tricks that make its success in my growing situation far more likely. (Remember, this is my experience alone; yours may be far different, even if you live just a block away!) Foxglove started from seed—that can survive to

be seedlings, and ultimately survive the difficult childhood of a biennial in Oklahoma—will grow into far more beautiful adulthood than those started from gallon plants in a nursery. Like everything planted in my garden, its ultimate success depends on getting established and gaining a foothold. For years, I tried to get them to colonize and do just that in a section of my backyard border. Directly in front of a climbing 'Gertrude Jekyll' rose, where it created a sublime color echo. In a perfect year, with perfect growing conditions (in other words, two or three out of the thirty years I have gardened here), this design plan worked well. It was all just as I imagined it would be. Consequently, I continue to try to replicate the look in this spot, albeit reservedly, every year since.

But most of the time now, I grow it where it seems to *want* to be in my landscape. In more shade, with less water, with less disruption from other plantings, and with greater wind protection. In my front garden beds, rather than the back. The quality of their performance changes from year to year, but in general, they do perform for me in this spot. In the front beds, the blooms are less colorful, shorter, and less dramatic with a more of a native quality to them, but that is okay. They are still beautiful and worthy of their spot in the garden. So says my heart, anyway, who runs the show in their regard.

BASIC GARDEN NEEDS

SOIL AND NUTRIENTS

Most plants want rich, loamy soil with good friability and excellent drainage, two words that strike terror in the hearts of all of us who garden in heavy clay. Soil, in general, is described by the amount of clay, sand, and silt it contains. Good loamy soil, the texture of dark chocolate cake with good friability, is the holy grail of dirt, a balanced mixture of all three (that never seems to occur naturally in any garden). The degree to which our soil contains these ingredients will determine its texture, nutrients, and drainage capabilities—and of course, our gardening successes and failures.

It is well worth the effort to find just the right environment for a plant at the outset. Consider light, airflow, drainage, and water needs.

Clay soil, like mine, is heavy, often nutrient dense, and does not drain well. Sandy soil with its large particles drains well but does not hold on to water and nutrients, which can leach out quickly. Both can be improved with the addition of copious amounts of organic matter such as compost, leaf mold, and worm castings. Still, it has been my experience that no matter how much organic matter and soil amendment I add to the soil, its default setting is still heavy clay, and it is constantly trying to revert to its original clay setting.

Silty soil, with particles between sand and clay in size, has high fertility, but it is fine and powdery in texture and can become easily saturated and waterlogged. My own garden, with the exception of raised beds in the potager, is definitely clay-like to silty on the soil spectrum, with the exception of one blissful area of the garden, now containing massive oakleaf hydrangeas. Why? This area happened to have been the location of the former resident's sand pile for the children—sand that was incorporated into my clay soil when I started my garden bed. Those in my neighborhood, which was built on the location of a long-ago golf course, who drew the lucky card of a home lot on a sand trap versus the fairway are likewise blessed with areas of better drainage and soil texture.

WATER

Although the question about how much water your plants really need is simple, the answer is not. When and how much water is optimal are among the most mysterious and elusive of garden answers to find, I think. Looking to "expert" sources for recommendations provide only guidelines at best. A smart gardener knows that his or her gardening microclimates, geography, season, and landscape situation are the driving factors in determining just how much water is really necessary, guidelines notwithstanding, to grow a beautiful and healthy garden.

SPACE AND AIRFLOW

One of the biggest mistakes I make in my own garden is to pay too little attention to the mature size of a plant before adding it to my garden. That petite quart-size plant may soon outgrow its space if you fail to heed the information on the plant tag. How large it will ultimately get at maturity is important to know at the outset. If you want it to succeed in your garden, give it the room it needs to spread its wings. While I believe in dense planting to serve as living mulch and to deter weeds, I also need to recognize that *things grow!* (Sadly, this obvious lesson is one I have to learn over and over again.) At least I hope they will, so why not give them the room to do so? Plus, lack of airflow, crucial to preventing disease and pest issues, can cause vexing problems for you and the garden in the future.

LIGHT

This may be the most straightforward, if not the easiest, of plant requirements to provide. Plant tags, seed packets, and reference sources provide good information about just how much shade or sun, indirect light, or exposure a plant needs to grow. I generally also find that gardeners always seem to want what they don't have. If they have a lot of shade, they want more sun. If too much sun, hence more shade. Both are sentiments completely understandable to gardeners who want to grow all varieties of plants and vegetables.

To a certain degree, this is in a gardener's control. Trees can be pruned to allow more light through the canopy. Raising the canopy of the tree by removing lower limbs and thinning out twiggy growth from major branches allows more light to penetrate below, while simultaneously often creating fabulous branching architecture. Of course, a tree can be removed completely to create the full sun exposure loved by so many flowers and vegetables. But often this is a difficult, expensive, and sometimes even an emotional decision. I find it helps to get several valued opinions before making a decision as major as this.

While symptoms of over- or underwatering can look remarkably similar and be difficult to diagnose, it's more obvious when a plant needs more or less sun and or light. In my own garden, I follow a "three strikes and you're out" system in matching a plant to its perfect exposure. In other words, I will locate

Above: *Rudbeckia laciniata*, the cutleaf coneflower, is a native to North America. It can be overly aggressive in a garden with too much moisture, but in my unirrigated bed, it minds its manners and produces sunny blooms in summer.

Opposite: The potager in the summer speaks to my own love of weathered brick, functional garden ornaments, and vertical accents for visual layering.

Definition of Light Exposure in the Garden

- Full Sun: six or more hours of direct sunlight per day
- Part Sun: four to six hours of direct sun per day
- Part Shade: four to six hours of sun per day, primarily before the heat of the day
- Full Shade: less than four hours of sun per day

a plant three times to help it find its "happy place" before I determine it simply doesn't want to live in my garden. Three strikes and you're out!

These are *very* general guidelines of course, and must be adapted, sometimes greatly, to your growing zone, average summer temperatures, and the density of the shade itself. Experimentation is the best course of action in determining how much sun a plant *really* wants in your garden.

No matter how carefully you try to calibrate soil, light, and water to your plant's specifications, usually Mother Nature has the last word. Together she and I have killed more than our share of flowers, shrubs, trees, and vegetables despite our best efforts to meet the needs of our garden plantings. In the end, I found that meeting the aesthetic needs of myself as the gardener *and* the cultural requirements of the plants in my garden was crucial to creating the beautiful, sensual garden that lived up to my ambitions. It turned out to be that simple, at least as a driving philosophy. To quote Coco Chanel, "Simplicity is the keynote of all true elegance."

Chapter 2

GARDEN STYLE AND SETTING

MAKE IT YOUR OWN

All of us are artists in one form or another. Our mediums of choice for artistic expression vary, of course, and make each one of us unique in our creative endeavors. My medium for personal expression—what I find fulfilling, evocative, and life-giving—is gardening and beautifying my outdoor living spaces. It is a way I can communicate my own sense of style, of personal likes and dislikes, and to a certain extent, even my value set and what is important to me. By looking at my garden as a work of art and a means of individual expression, I find the garden transcends horticulture, collecting plants, and implementing a design. Indeed, I find that I look at almost everything through a gardening lens and it is no cliche to say that living a true *garden lifestyle* is very important to me and, I think, a form of artistry in its own right.

To me, creating an elegant garden that manifests, reinforces, and communicates my particular style and look is a matter of careful curation done over a period of time—curating an identifiable *signature look* through careful additions, and, as importantly, through subtractions and thoughtful editing. I have been building and molding my own garden for over thirty years, and in that time, it has changed and been transfigured right along with me. I made changes (and sometimes changes were brutally imposed by Mother Nature) based on my lifestyle and evolving tastes, my family's needs, major weather events, a changing climate, and the availability of resources. As

You can't fight Mother Nature. Always try to work with her at your side. This *Cleome* 'Inncleosr' Senorita Rosalita®, *Hylotelephium* 'Herbstfreude' Autumn Joy®, and annual salvias grow well in my Oklahoma garden, even facing south, and are pollinator magnets.

I learn more about garden styles and am exposed to more and different kinds of gardens, my preferences and what I find appealing evolves, morphs, and ultimately informs my garden aesthetic, thus dictating more changes and updates. That is to say, my garden and my personal expression of it is very dynamic, ever changing, and not created in a vacuum. It was and is contextual. Our gardens are in constant dialogue with us as its caretakers and the environment in which we cultivate it.

GOOD "GARDEN FIT"

CONTEXT: *The situation in which something happens, and that can help explain it.*

—The Cambridge Dictionary

As an example of what I mean about context, let me share the context of my own garden and the specifics of my personal garden circumstances and setting. What I am aiming for is what I call a *Good Garden Fit*. A beautiful garden that fits within the context of where I live and how I garden. As I go through this exercise as it relates to my garden, try to do the same as it pertains to your garden environment.

MY CONSIDERATIONS FOR
GOOD GARDEN FIT

- NEIGHBORHOOD: I garden in an urban historic preservation area amongst older homes built in the 1930s. I am required to get approval before making certain changes to the exterior of my home and property. Homes are relatively close together and share a common vintage and decorum, if not architectural style. What I do in my front landscape can affect the look, health, and even the marketability of homes on my street.
- FAMILY: My two boys are now grown and have moved out. I am an empty nester and no longer need to allocate large sections of the landscape to their high-energy play or sections of the potager to their culinary preferences. While supportive, my husband doesn't garden, and I do the majority of the work myself. At this stage of my life, I want to enjoy the garden more and maintain it less. My garden budget may be larger now that my sons are out of college and I am working full time, but I am by nature thrifty and always cognizant of the value of a dime.
- GEOGRAPHY: I garden in prairie soil with extreme heat in the summer and, sometimes, extreme cold, ice, and snow in the winter. These extremes are getting *more* extreme over time. Recently, in late winter, my state experienced an extreme, rapid temperature shift in just three days.

Because of its steeply pitched roof, topiary forms, and abundant plantings, my Tudor home is often called "the fairy tale house."

My city and state are in the most drought-prone section of the country, and we are often on water rationing. We contend with high wind, frequent ice and hailstorms, and when it does rain, it often comes all at once. As the weather becomes more extreme, the continuum of plants I can easily grow seems to be shrinking. I rely more heavily on tough, reliable, and, yes, sometimes more ordinary, steadfast plants that have stood the test of time and difficult growing conditions. I am continually trying to romance the ordinary into something special and extraordinary.

- LIFESTYLE: I prefer to garden more intensely in the fall and spring, less so in the heat of the summer. More and more, I am prioritizing lower maintenance and more drought-tolerant plantings. I prefer morning to afternoon and evening in the garden for both working and entertaining. I think of my garden spaces as extensions of my home. I like a tidy, well-kept look year-round, if possible.
- INTERESTS AND PRIORITIES: I want a garden for entertaining and outdoor living, with a heavy concentration on container plantings and fresh ingredients for the kitchen and vase.

I am increasingly fascinated with the concept of edible landscaping and using edibles as ornamentals. I am more interested in texture, shape, and form than color and bloom. I love growing plants but am more interested in plants relative to a design objective than plants as individual specimens to grow and collect.

- HOME: I live in a 1932 English Tudor home of brick and stone with a very highly pitched roof and large, semi-enclosed porch. The architectural lines are curved and arched rather than linear and straight. It sits on a relatively small lot of 0.21 acres (0.08 hectares). All the neighborhood backyards are enclosed with fencing. Houses and neighbors are in close vicinity, and privacy for all is always a consideration. My home is often called the "fairy tale house" because of its architecture and surrounding garden, and I try to emphasize its charm in this respect. It is in a very walkable neighborhood that gets lots of seasonal traffic during the peak gardening seasons.

In developing your own personal garden style, I would first recommend going through this same exercise in relation to all these elements. How do they pertain to your own individual set of gardening circumstances and the context and parameters of where you garden? Considering *all* these factors will take some of the frustration out of selecting what communicates *your* personal garden style amongst so many style options and trends available in gardening.

In addition, it can't be overstated the degree to which considering these garden "givens" will create and provide visual harmony with the surrounding landscape or neighborhood and reduce optic tension (and sometimes inter-neighbor tension) between incompatible elements and factors related to gardening in your specific area. Simply put, by making decisions that are contextual to your garden location, you are *simultaneously* making it personal

My own personal style expresses itself in strong, rounded, clipped forms, lots of texture, and a restrained use of color.

This stunning potager designed by Paul Hendershot Design is called "East Coast Style" no doubt because it so perfectly fits into the setting and geography where it is located.

In a small garden like mine, I pack in herbs, annuals, and other plants wherever I can—in containers large and small, and in layers using hanging baskets and plant stands. I consider this layered effect part of my signature style.

and expressing your garden's personality with less effort, more enjoyment, and in a language that speaks to your home's architecture, neighborhood, land, geography, and your unique gardening voice.

SIGNATURE STYLE AND SIGNATURE TOUCHES

If it seems as if I am constantly prying you with questions so far, it is because developing a "look" and garden style begins with asking the overarching question: *How do I get from here to there to achieve the look I want?* and then continually asking yourself what you like and what can work within your per-

sonal life situation to get there. Consider it the best form of gardening introspection and self-absorption with no downside. Horticultural matchmaking of the best kind! Graphically, here's how that looks:

Before you realize it, you will have a garden that is uniquely and identifiably your own, regardless of your growing circumstances. Over time and through multiple iterations and weather events, you will have created a garden that is recognizable as *yours* with your own personality and individual garden panache.

When I first started to garden, and when my boys were in elementary school, I remember becoming

Johnny and Jamie's mother. At that point in time, that's how I was identified, and I was proud to be so. Fast forward to recent years, when numerous people drive by and recognize my garden and home from tours, social media, or magazines before they recognize or identify *me* working in the front beds. Passers-by screech to a halt to tell me they recognized my garden and its unique look and personality. I am now known as the lady in the historic old neighborhood with an English garden on the Oklahoma prairie—and I am proud to be so. They recognize it, I hope, because of the unique and unexpected details they see in my garden but don't see in a lot of others or in the same combination. And by virtue of social media, images, and information about my garden that can be found all over the world on YouTube, Instagram, and my website, making it even more identifiable.

Identifying, defining, and exploring signature touches for your garden is one of the most satisfying, revelatory, and fun aspects of creating a garden that is distinctly and uniquely your own. In addition, deconstructing gardens you visit in this same way will help unlock the mysteries of those gardens and answer this question: *Now why does it look and feel the way it does?*

A friend of mine who was a local television news anchor for many years was quite emphatic about one of her signature touches—she only wanted white and green in her garden. Despite my encouragement to add a touch of lavender here or pale pink there, she stuck to her sophisticated palette, and her garden is that much more personal and beautiful because of it. She later explained to me it was because she only had time to enjoy her garden after nightfall when she got home after the 10 p.m. newscast.

My friend Roger has a distinctive color palette as well. He limits what he grows to yellow, lavender, blue, white, and green. In his very particular growing situation, he has the luxury of being able to embrace low-growing invasives (something most of us avoid, no matter how beautiful the garden thug is) without regret, as he explains it. Ground covers and self-seeders that may be overly aggressive in others' gardens are welcome in his unirrigated

garden where he can easily keep them in check. Verbena *(Verbena bonariensis)*, Queen Anne's lace *(Daucus carota)*, arugula *(Eruca vesicaria ssp. sativa)*, parsley (*Petroselinum crispum*), dill (*Anethum graveolens*), larkspur (*Delphinium*), cypress spurge (*Euphorbia cyparissias*), native asters (*Symphyotrichum*), and goldenrod (*Solidago*) are all at liberty (with some exceptions) to plant themselves wherever they choose. Architectural salvage pieces are used as focal points throughout the landscape, punctuating different areas of the garden along with massive boxwood balls and hidden container plantings and water features. It is a wonderful world of novelty, botanical surprises, fascinating plant

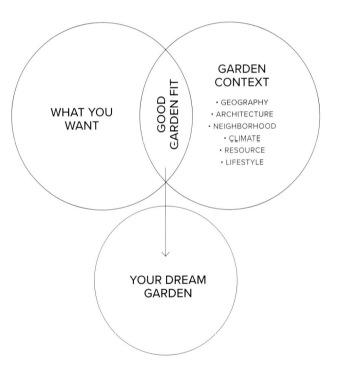

The intersection of "What You Want" and your personal "Garden Context" will help you determine the "Good Garden Fit" of "Your Dream Garden."

Circle 1: What You Want The universe of *everything* you like, love, and want in your garden, landscape, and outdoor living areas.

Circle 2: Garden Context What can succeed and is practical within your specific garden context and resource limitations as they exist *now*, recognizing these will change over time. These resources may be environmental, financial, spatial, labor- and/or age-related, and time-based.

The intersection of these two spaces is your world of possibilities to create . . .

Circle 3: Your Dream Garden in the now with good "Garden Fit" achievability and your own special touches.

combinations, and unusual, rustic garden orna-ments—a welcoming place for humans and avian and insect wildlife. It is a whole world filled with his signature touches.

Personal garden statements and signature touches need not be limited to what is visual, of course. Another friend of mine thinks that a plant without fragrance is hardly worth cultivating and sipping tea or wine in her garden on an evening with a gentle breeze is nothing short of heavenly. Yet another gardener I know is fascinated with ginkgo *(Ginkgo biloba)* cultivars and has an excep-tional collection of bonsai scattered throughout his fabulous garden.

A wide range of possibilities exist to help us make our gardens singular and special. With the right approach and uniquely personal sensibilities, uncommon beauty and garden mastery can be cultivated from the most common of materials and

Signature Touches

Those elements that make your garden and home uniquely and distinctively yours— that help you express and create your own recognizable garden personality, style, and identity in and out of the garden.

plants. Consider it *romancing the ordinary*.

It's one of the reasons I find topiary so compelling, and probably the most recognizable of my own signature touches. It lends dramatic signature appointments to my garden spaces, is meditative and soothing, and is a great source of immediate gratification.

Ten Signature Touches in My Garden

Objectives: to achieve garden romance without sweetness; handsome, good looks over time versus constant flowering abundance; and harmony and rhythm over contrast and visual discord.

- Highly manicured grass edge.
- Use of brick and stone as edging, decking, and pathway.
- Containers placed inside the garden beds and extensive use of topiary in pots and in garden beds.
- Heavy reliance on clipped evergreens, especially boxwood.
- Extensive layering in and out of garden beds using both plant material and garden structures and ornament.
- Garden accessories tend to be organic in material and are aged, weathered, and mossy with an old, established garden look.
- Trees are sculpted and pruned high with an open canopy to provide high, dappled shade.

- Heavy use of seasonal color is limited to spring and fall.
- Using edibles as ornamentals in the land-scape, and vice versa.
- Use of gravel as flooring and to mulch some beds and containers.

Manifesto

A written statement declaring publicly the intentions, motives, or view of its issuer.
—Merriam Webster

CREATE A GARDENING MANIFESTO

Creating my own gardening manifesto was one of the most fun and helpful exercises I ever put together. In my experience as a gardener, I discovered that no matter how long I have gardened, nor how experienced a gardener I have become, I continually have to learn the same lessons over and over again. Writing down my own driving motivations, reminders, and best practices helps me stay on track and take the long view. It also is a helpful comfort when the weather gods deal my garden yet another blow. It reminds me that both the garden and the gardener are resilient and adaptable. I often tell new gardeners that *to garden is to suffer*. The sooner we accept this reality, the more equanimity and perspective we have. As with our family and friends, it is those things we love the most that can cause the greatest heartaches. Like the garden, my garden manifesto is a living, breathing, changing thing. I tweak it a bit each year as I grow older and wiser and face new gardening challenges and opportunities. I have it displayed prominently, and when I finally have that garden shed and greenhouse that I am dreaming of for my next garden, it will hold centerstage—framed and at eye level.

Garden Manifesto

Gardening is so important to me that I wrote out my own garden manifesto, a written recitation of my views, motives, observations, and policies related to gardening. It's a fun exercise to do, and I encourage everyone who loves gardening to compose one for themselves.

1. Don't let your plants boss you.
2. There are only two seasons, before the heat and after the heat.
3. A little bit every day beats a torn disk and backbreaking labor later.
4. Procrastination in the garden, especially when it relates to pests, is a big no-no.
5. There are three major opportunity points: before a rain, after a rain, and as seasons transition.
6. Gardens should match the style and architecture of the home and speak the same language.
7. Make your garden match your personal lifestyle, not the other way around.
8. A garden without life and movement is not a garden. It's a stage set.
9. Gardens are ever changing, dynamic organisms. Try to embrace and work WITH the garden. Don't fight it.
10. Always, always, always remember context. What climate you're in, what neighborhood you're in, what season you're in.
11. S*** happens. Don't take it personally and try not to beat yourself up about it. To be a gardener is to suffer. There is always the next season. The next year.
12. Embrace your inner kindergartner. Never lose the joy and excitement of a seed germinating, a flower finally blooming, and the miracles made by Mother Nature.

TOPIARY

I'm not sure exactly when my topiary addiction began. It might have been when I clipped my first boxwood ball as an endcap to the box hedge in the parterre of the potager. I found the way its simple spherical shape punctuated the entry points toward the center of the design imminently satisfying. That globular form somehow manages to express multiple traits simultaneously—softness with its rounded shape, yet strong geometry and architecture with its tightly clipped form. It communicates both whimsy and sophistication at the same time. Truly, it *is* living sculpture—horticulture, art form, and a delightful hobby.

Soon boxwood balls, in harmonic rhythm and repetition, were planted and pruned like so many bocce balls tossed across the landscape. My affection for this shape didn't stop with boxwood. Tightly clipped evergreens of all sorts became fodder for

Opposite: A topiary can be created out of a wide variety of plants. This small sampling contains topiary made from lemon cypress (*Hesperocyparis macrocarpa* 'Goldcrest'), dwarf cotoneaster, 'Compacta' dwarf myrtle (*Myrtus communis* 'Compacta'), and boxwood.

Above: A multi-generational topiary family reunion of 'Compacta' dwarf myrtle takes place each summer in my backyard where they thrive with lots of water and full sun. But never let them dry out completely, or they will likely not recover!

my shears, and inevitably herbs such as rosemary, lavender, basil, thyme, and germander (*Teucrium chamaedrys*) entered the picture. As I experimented with other plants, I also began to experiment with other classic shapes for topiary, especially container topiary, both for the garden and for the tabletop. While I have little interest in creating fanciful animal creatures or storybook characters, my affection for different simple geometric shapes has grown. A simple lollipop form—a ball on a single trunk, a.k.a.,

a standard—remains my favorite. Poodle varieties with double, triple, or more spheres on a single trunk are fun to grow and amusing to look at. After all, a ball on a stick has the primal charm and appeal of how a child draws their first tree—simple, straightforward, and elegant in its innocent restraint. I especially love to display my topiaries as a collection, displayed in groups that migrate between home and garden for holiday display, interior decor, or table centerpieces.

Opposite: Pots filled with boxwood topiaries march up and down the steps leading to my back door. Wire vine (*Muehlenbeckia axillaris*) and lady's mantle (*Alchemilla mollis*) spill out over the edges. Various succulents complete the scene.

Right: Snipping plants into topiary forms is not only a creative expression, but a gardening form of meditation and mindfulness for me.

Plants used for topiaries are typically evergreen with woody stems; have small needles, leaves, or foliage; have a dense growing habit when frequently pruned; and have a compact or vertically upright and/or columnar growth pattern. That said, I have seen *magnificent* specimens created out of fleshy and flowering plants. Think basil, coleus (*Coleus scutellarioides*), scented geraniums (*Pelargonium*), lantana (*Lantana camara*), fuchsia (*Fuchsia*), roses, and hydrangeas (*Hydrangea macrophylla*).

Despite its sophisticated reputation, a topiary can be created out of even the most common and inexpensive of plant materials and need not be costly. I often shop my own garden for topiary candidates: small junipers (*Juniperus*) or laurels (*Laurus nobilis*) that have volunteered in my garden or been planted by birds or squirrels, cuttings of boxwood that unexpectedly took root after trimming the hedge in the potager, or divisions or cuttings of herbs such as rosemary (*Salvia rosmarinus*) and germander (*Teucrium chamaedrys*) from the potager that start small but mature into beautiful specimens over time. For the impatient, wire forms in classic shapes can be used to create "instant" topiary. A wire wreath circle magically becomes topiary when long stems of fragrant rosemary, thyme, or wire vine are encouraged to wind around the circular shape. Standard ball-on-stem wire forms, in singular or multiple ball shapes, look impressive almost immediately when a hanging basket of ivy with long tendrils is planted at the base and then trained up the metal "trunk."

Obviously, however you start them, depending on the scale and ambition of your topiary project, creating and training a topiary takes patience, a good eye for selecting a topiary to shape, and a steady hand. But, most importantly, I have found creating and transforming a shrub into a topiary form requires simple bravery, sharp shears, and an attitude that one really can't make a mistake. The worst haircuts ultimately grow out, after all. If I see a $6 shrub at my local nursery that has topiary potential, I am eager to get my shears on it—and if it doesn't immediately manifest the form I envision, I consider it a gardening risk well worth taking!

If patience is not your strong suit, or you want the immediate drama of a large topiary specimen in your garden, consider buying one ready made in topiary form. These can be pricey, of course, but for those of us who prefer such things over diamonds or furs—or even regular manicures—the expense for instant maturity is worth it. Well-stocked independent nurseries will usually have a selection, but be on the lookout even at home improvement, grocery, and hardware stores for good deals, especially at peak season and during the holidays.

TOPIARY CARE AND CULTIVATION

Like any type of plant care, watering, fertilizing, pruning, meeting light requirements, and winterizing topiaries depends on the plant material you are using and the size of the container in which it is grown. Many of my topiaries, notably my tabletop myrtle collection, my large eugenias, bay tree, olive trees, and rosemary are not hardy or only marginally so. Consequently, I have to bring them indoors or overwinter them at a friend's greenhouse. This is not an inconsequential consideration if you are hoping to grow large specimens that are not cold tolerant.

Many of my tabletop topiaries, especially those in small pots, require frequent (sometimes as much as twice a day, depending on summer heat) watering. Small pots dry out quite quickly, even with a topdressing of mulch and some protection from sun and wind. Frequent watering means more frequent feeding, as watering leaches out nutrients more quickly. I have found that moving topiary in the garden to a more amenable location, as the seasons change and the sun moves, helps ensure happy plants when weather conditions become extreme.

Making Topiaries

When looking for a candidate to form a classic ball on stem standard, try to identify plants with a strong, straight, central stem or trunk. This can require lifting up the skirts of foliage to see what branching architecture lies underneath. Sometimes plants in the nursery that are lanky, skinny, and sad looking make the best topiary as fullness is not what you are searching for—rather a strong central stem and good high branching.

If a globe is what you hope to sculpt, then a round full form is your objective. Finding a specimen that already tends to grow in this manner will speed the process of growing a mature topiary sphere.

Left: Lavender makes a beautiful if not particularly long-lived topiary. I buy them whenever I see them at the beginning of the growing season—usually around Easter where I live. Grown to look their best at purchase, lavender topiaries often have trouble transitioning past spring. In that case, I enjoy and care for them as long as they last. If they expire, I thank them for their service and relegate them to the compost pile in the sky. At purchase, they are no more costly than a large bouquet of flowers. Even if they don't make it through the summer, they last considerably longer than those bouquet blooms would last and for no more money!

Below: Tabletop myrtle topiaries and delicate pelargoniums look elegant staged in an outdoor seating area I have dubbed "the Bistro."

STYLISH GARDEN ACCOUTREMENT: THE STUFF OF GARDENS

My husband is a fly fisherman, and he loves nothing better than being at the riverside with a fly rod in hand, casting for trout on a beautiful day. When he is not fishing, he likes to read about fishing, plan his next fishing trip, and play with his fishing stuff—flies and lures, vests and waders, rods and reels, nets, and knives. Gardeners, does this infatuation with a hobby's accoutrement sound somewhat familiar?

Ah, the allure of gardening accessories! Both for you the garden caretaker, and the garden itself. Chicken wire cloches and metal tuteurs—I'll take them! Mossy pots, weatherproof baskets, wood-handled trowels with matching pruners? Who can resist? We gardeners love the stuff of gardening almost as much as we love the plants themselves, and these garden accessories can help immensely in establishing our own signature style and garden aesthetic. How and where we use them contributes immeasurably to our look and creates great synergy between plants and garden ornaments, especially when the ornament is both functional and beautiful.

Here are a few examples of how different gardeners achieve different moods via statement-making garden accoutrements. By changing garden accessories and garden ornaments, we can change the mood, the tone, the energy, and the language of the garden. Plants and gardens are by their very nature changing and ephemeral. Blooms come and go along with the seasons. Decorative garden adornments can too, and they need not be staid, permanent, and stuffy. Such is the magic of private over public gardens, where temporary displays of plants and objects communicate the personality of both the gardener and the seasons. Blending stylish accents in your own unique way truly makes your garden spaces personal. Indeed, nothing communicates how you express your own gardening lifestyle more than things you use to showcase it. Here are some image examples of garden styles that have

A large painted wooden cloche is the ultimate garden accessory as it serves to protect tender lettuces from hungry bunnies, serves as a brilliant focal point, and creates happy contrast to the surrounding greenery.

a very specific look but can also overlap in their application in the garden.

Quite often it's not another plant you need to set off a space, but a reflective surface, eye-catching sculpture, artfully placed finials, or a well-positioned birdbath. Just remember, too much of anything—even a good thing—is still too much. Tread the line carefully between accessorizing and cluttering.

STYLE I: ORGANIC, EARTHY, NATURAL, UNOBTRUSIVE

A woodpile has an earthy appeal that is attractive, is inexpensive, and effectively divides this space, while providing a beautiful deep brown backdrop to these vibrant geraniums. The geraniums are planted in a concrete faux bois planter that speaks the same earthy vibe. A small stone fireplace off to the side completes the scene.

STYLE II: ARTISTIC, COLORFUL, DRAMATIC FOCAL POINTS

Walls of arching bamboo in my friends Rob and Jim's garden frame the view to this glass sculpture and retro metal chairs in the distance.

STYLE III: COTTAGEY, CLASSIC, CHARMING

This white cottage complete with string lights and flowering porch rail boxes says welcome in a most endearing way. It's a classic look that can't go wrong.

STYLE IV: SLEEK, MODERN, INDUSTRIAL, LINEAR

Metal posts, wood rectilinear raised beds, and clean lines communicate an industrial, streamlined aura. These containers are in a natural setting and look perfectly at home but would look equally as comfortable in a modern residential setting.

STYLE V: ROMANTIC, FEMININE

This window box on the front of my house is filled with the romance of tulips, trailing ivies, and pansies. Extra pots, baskets, and topiary add to the feminine vibe. It's also an instance where two styles interface: cottage meets romantic.

I love the texture and personality of using baskets and woven elements in the garden. I designed these flexible, waterproof, weatherproof versions for QVC when I couldn't source them elsewhere.

CONTAINERS

Opposite: Galvanized metal chicken wire cloches stand ready to protect emerging seedlings, and black metal plant supports or tuteurs frame *Ligustrum* 'Sunshine,' which will soon fill the cages and form fit their elegant lines.

Right: This mossy pot screams "I am part of an old, established estate garden with lots of help and a large garden staff!" At least that's what I am hearing.

Below: Nothing communicates your garden style more than your choice of containers. Does your garden speak the language of terracotta, concrete, metal, or glazed pottery? Though all beautiful, show restraint in the variety of materials you use, lest it look too messy, cluttered, and disorganized.

TOOLS

Top: Garden accessories are for the gardener as well as the garden—for both working in the garden and for "après gardening." Garden attire is a fun way to express your personality in and out of the landscape.

Bottom: How a gardener manages his or her tools is a highly personal thing. Sadly, no matter how good looking my tool bag is, it doesn't prevent me from leaving and losing prized garden instruments in the garden.

Opposite: The tulips may outshine the birdbath and topiaries in this spring tableau, but when the tulips die back, and their vibrant color along with them, the concrete birdbath will hold center stage as a focal point in all the summer green.

PART II **INSPIRATION**

"THE GARDEN MUST FIRST BE PREPARED IN THE
SOUL OR ELSE IT WILL NOT FLOURISH."
—ENGLISH PROVERB

Chapter 3

GARDEN DESIGN

FORMULATE A PLAN

If you are an amateur gardener like me, you may find the word *design* itself intimidating. It might conjure up painful memories of a hated geometry class, terms like parabola, arc, and radius, not to mention graph paper, measuring tools and, yes, dollar signs. But in actuality, this can be one of the most exciting phases of the process of creating an edible garden. Much of designing your garden spaces is intuitive, channeling things that you already know and have seen—things that are obvious, that make perfect sense aesthetically and practically, and that you see examples of everywhere you look. On many levels, you *already* know how to design your edible garden.

Your plan and its direction will of course be informed by the answers to the questions you asked yourself in chapters 1 and 2. Answers that relate to garden style, preferences, and your personal wish list. To execute your plan, I suggest following certain principles of garden design, be it on a large or small scale, that will make the process easier and obvious. These principles include:

- Enclosure
- Entry
- Framing the View
- Focal Point

- Structure
- Color
- Texture

- Pattern
- Rhythm
- Repetition

These principles apply to the largest and smallest of gardens. Whether on a terrace or an estate, they up the sophistication ante of any garden space and enhance the experience of the end user of the garden.

As an example, let me use my own potager and the mental process I followed to formulate my design plan, in relation to these principles, before even one measurement was taken or one plant was selected. But first things first. Using my own intuition and inspiration from places I had visited and seen, I had to decide where I wanted to put it.

Practical matters such as sunlight, proximity to my kitchen, and proximity to water had to be considered. Once those issues were addressed, I could put my intuition and knowledge into an actionable design plan to make it work aesthetically with my home and landscape. As Nicole Johnsey Burke says in her book *Kitchen Garden Revival*, it's about balancing priorities and practical consider- ations, with no location being 100 percent perfect. Remember, we have to design and execute our plans within a set of givens that we don't always have control over.

To determine the exact location of my own kitchen garden, I gathered all my photos, my notes, my impressions, and my wish list from my visit to Barnsley House. I knew I wanted a destination gar- den, a place to get away both in mood and location, with a sense of being its own garden room and a dedicated kitchen garden space. This is an English gardening concept I love and wanted to emulate. I also wanted a small parterre with boxwood hedging to contain and divide the plantings. Consequently, it had to be spacious enough and with enough sun exposure to support its health and good looks.

A rendering of my backyard with its distinctive garden rooms. The potager on the right side of the detached garage-studio shows a naturally enclosed space to exploit.

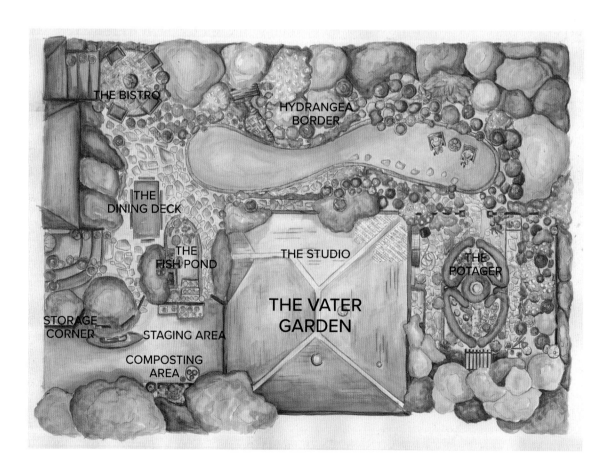

THE BISTRO

HYDRANGEA BORDER

THE DINING DECK

THE FISH POND

THE STUDIO

THE POTAGER

THE VATER GARDEN

STORAGE CORNER

STAGING AREA

COMPOSTING AREA

Parterre

A level space in a garden or yard occupied by an ornamental, formal arrangement of beds and paths to form a pattern. The borders of the beds may be defined with tightly clipped hedging, stone, brick, or other material. The beds themselves may be filled with planted pots, flowers, vegetables, herbs, or topiary, or left empty with just mulch or gravel and a statement garden fixture.

My potager is a destination garden, separate and away from the back of my home. I walk the length of my backyard and beyond the studio and take a right turn into the potager.

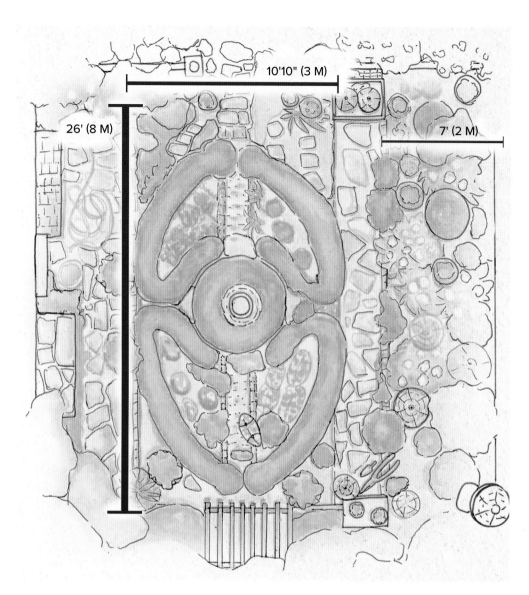

10'10" (3 M)

26' (8 M)

7' (2 M)

Above: The dimensions of my garden dictated the shape and the scale of its elements—the path, beds, planting zones, and hedging—making its design easier from the outset.

Opposite: This view of the potager clearly shows the sides of my enclosed space: the fences on the north and east sides, the entry, and the studio from which the picture was taken.

It is easy to see from this diagram and aerial view of my small urban garden that options were limited, but also obvious. The first time I saw my house and its surroundings, I *intuited* and simply noticed that a secret garden, perhaps a *kitchen garden*, of some kind could be perfectly located behind the detached garage and in front of the fence on the east and north side—a naturally enclosed space.

Happily, it had good sun exposure, easy access to water, and was distanced from the house, but not inconveniently so. Consequently, a perfect spot for my edible garden. Coincidentally, it also addressed, at least partially, the first of the small garden design principles that are so important in creating a successful garden space.

ENCLOSURE

A sense of intimacy is very important to me both in and out of the garden. I find it absolutely essential in establishing the personality and temper of my garden. It is why I was drawn to this circumscribed space as the location for my potager. It has a feeling of privacy, security, and coziness within its confines.

This feeling of containment communicates a number of things to the gardener and its visitors. First, it divides a larger landscape into smaller contained sections such that each enclosed area doesn't seem intimidatingly large—too large to manage the work and cultivation of what is required in its boundaries. I could hear myself saying, *"Today, I will tackle this room of the garden,"* just as I would divide and tackle the chores related to cleaning different rooms of my home. It automatically implies a division of labor that made sense to me and seemed doable with a clearly defined beginning and end. This is particularly true in the torrid summer months of a southern garden, when marathon gardening is neither safe nor possible. To this day, the partitioning and separation of both garden spaces and garden toil help me manage the workload and maintenance of the gardens. It gives me a sense of control and prevents feelings of being overwhelmed.

Secondly, feeling "hugged" by the existing walls and fences gives me a sense of security and privacy that I find comforting on the most anxious of days. I feel hidden and protected from the world as I cut flowers or pick radishes in my pajamas in the morning.

Enclosed gardens also feel solid and attached and anchored to place, fortressed from what surrounds them. This sense of permanence in a landscape design can be as comforting as its aura

Secretly Getting a Glimpse of the Garden

Still, one can never fully escape the prying eyes of determined gardeners. A few years ago, as I was working in my potager and thinking that I was concealed from view, I heard quiet chattering overhead—above and behind me slightly to the west to be exact. There, dressed in ladies-do-lunch attire, were four women teetering on heels in the tree house belonging to the neighbor children who lived behind me. While I could see them, they could not see me. I overheard one of them say they "just had to get a peek of what the back looked like, since the front was so lovely." Had they asked, I would have happily shown them the back gardens, but perhaps it was much more thrilling to scale the ladder of a tree house to spy on a secret garden. A sentiment I can completely relate to. Gardening brings out the kid in all of us. If you wonder if I ever revealed myself, no I did not—for fear of scaring them and toppling them like well-dressed Humpty Dumpties from their perch! They were, after all, gardeners after my own heart, and I think of them fondly to this day.

By enclosing this small kitchen garden inside a rough cedar and hog wire fence, the homeowner, my friend Elaine, created a garden room in an otherwise open space. In designing this garden, careful measuring ensured the gate passage was wide enough to accommodate a wheelbarrow. Planter boxes on stilts divide beds and help manage planting, labor, and harvest with little bending required.

The parterre in the potager is divided into five sections, each enclosed by the 'Wintergreen' boxwood hedge. Four symmetrical sections surround a circle in the center of the design.

of safety and retreat—a haven from the rest of the world. In my situation, the enclosure speaks to my home and landscape with brick walls, fencing, arbors, and the natural contours of my property.

But gardens can also be enclosed within living walls—hedges of evergreens or expanses of trellis with climbing vines. Think of the massive yew hedges in English gardens, boxwood in colonial America, or the totemic privet privacy hedges in the Hamptons.

More modest and informal enclosures can be created with groupings of large pots on a deck to surround the corners or edges of a pool, or by filling empty niches on a porch. Temporary "walls" of container plantings also can serve as moveable screens throughout the seasons as the sun moves or the

wind changes. Permeable structures permit good airflow and a gentle breeze, pleasant for garden visitors and essential to preventing diseases, pesky mosquitoes, and pests in your plantings that demand good air circulation.

ENCLOSURE WITHIN ENCLOSURE: ORGANIZED CHAOS

This idea of enclosure also can be applied to the plantings themselves within an enclosed garden space. For example, the boxwood knot garden in my potager enclosed by the house and fence is divided into four quadrants with a circle in the center, areas which I have cleverly named Quadrants 1, 2, 3, and 4. Four tidy enclosures within the larger enclosed kitchen garden. I love the simple straightforward elegance of this arrangement.

Plants for Tightly Pruned Hedges

(Consider climate, rate of growth, and amount of light)

- Boxwood
- Rosemary
- Germander
- Dwarf yaupon holly
- Inkberry holly
- Blueberry
- Abelia
- Japanese euonymus
- Lavender
- Japanese pittosporum
- Sweet olive
- Distylium

As seen in my own garden, a thoughtfully curated group of pots can be placed anywhere to divide large areas and create a sense of enclosure.

Enclosure Fundamentals

- Enclosures provide a sense of intimacy, protection, and privacy.
- Enclosure helps divide the garden into manageable spaces for maintenance and organization.
- Enclosures reinforce the idea of garden rooms, with doorways, walls, and floors.
- Enclosures give definition to a space and help define its role, tone, and place in the garden.
- Enclosures relate in style and in execution to the entire garden by containing and unifying.
- Enclosures take into account airflow, circulation, and movement in and around the enclosed space.
- Enclosures can block wind, protect vulnerable plants, and buffer noise.

This division of the four areas defined and enclosed by the boxwood hedge helps in many ways to aid in planning my plantings, crop rotations, seasonal and daily labor, and garden goals. Over a period of four days, I can prune each one of the 'Wintergreen' boxwood quadrants, amend the soil in the interior, and then plant, groom, or seed each area consecutively. This divides the labor over time, gives me a sense of accomplishment and orderly progress, and saves my back from overuse in the process. I even love the pleasing tension between the clipped and kempt quadrants and those unpruned, fluffy ones yet to be tackled. In gardening, even the simplest of observations can be imminently satisfying. Consequently, the design concept and application of enclosure in your landscape provides psychological, emotional, practical, and aesthetic merit that is invaluable to both the garden and the gardener.

ENTRY

We all want to feel special and important, do we not? And that, in a nutshell, is why we want to pay special attention to points of entry in our gardens and the quality of the welcome we create for ourselves and our garden guests. Let's throw out the green carpet and give a hearty welcome to those who enter our garden spaces by thinking about the experience of entering our garden rooms and defined areas.

At certain times of the year and of the day, when the garden is at its most beautiful and the light is at its loveliest, my goal for the backyard entrance is to elicit an audible gasp from those who enter my back garden. I will ever so slowly open the arched gate to reveal the majesty of what the garden looks like at that specific moment in time. More often than not, I achieve my objective, as visitors—especially those seeing my garden for the first time—experience its beauty through that carefully thought-out portal into my garden world. From the squeaking of the garden gate to the way the light hits the edges of my large box topiary just so, to the contours of the wooden gate itself and the careful positioning of the display of plants the visitor sees unfold before them, no sensual element is overlooked to provide a grand entrance for my garden guests. Is the entrance this magical with each opening of the gate? No. That often depends on Mother Nature, not me. But it is always handsome, welcoming, and experientially pleasing if not gasp-inducing.

I often refer to what I think of as my "Theory of Garden Relativity" (on page 90) when planning my points of entry. This is my mental construct and guiding philosophy that everything in the garden relates to everything else in and about the garden. It is a constant dialogue that takes place between each and every garden element, whether botanical, structural, hardscape, or garden ornament in nature.

This is especially true when it comes to designing the entry to your garden spaces.

A grand home in a grand context will by its nature demand a grand entrance. But my garden is charming and modest in scale and in personality, so the gates, arbors, steps, pillars, containers, and features that constitute entry points are appropriate to its English Tudor character. The role of entry points in my garden is to communicate in a language consistent with my landscape and home that a change of some sort is imminent. The garden traveler is on the verge of entering a garden space with a different role, mood, location, or aspect in relation to the garden as a whole. An effective entry design will make this transition special and welcoming, whether dramatic or subtle in its execution.

Romantic gardens rely heavily on the use of billowing roses and other climbers, like blue virginsbower (*Clematis occidentalis*), honeysuckle (*Lonicera*), and high-climbing edibles like runner beans (*Phaseolus coccineus*), gourds (*Curcurbita*), peas (*Pisum sativum)*, and vigorous tomatoes (*Solanum lycopersicum*) to adorn arbors, pergolas, and fences that frame the entrance structures. When I built a wooden arbor, stained to match the trim of my home, as an entrance to my own potager, I planted a pink rambling 'Climbing Old Blush' rose on the short fence attached to it. On the arbor itself, a fragrant 'Zephirine Drouhin' rose—a thornless climber that is a joy to train—was planted as well, also in pink, creating a romantic entry worthy of any Jane Austen novel. Looking through this flowery entrance to the boxwood hedge of the potager with its encased herbs and vegetables beyond is one of the true joys of my spring and early summer garden. Sadly, they have both succumbed to the dreaded rose rosette disease (a viral condition spread by tiny mites that causes roses to grow strangely deformed stems, leaves, and flowers), but I am already planning other treasures to fill the space. Truly, a garden is an ever-changing organism!

Opposite: This arbor into my kitchen garden demonstrates all the important design principles: enclosure, entry, framing the view, focal point, structure, color, texture, pattern, rhythm, and repetition.

On a late summer evening, visitors who come through my back gate are greeted by this view of sculpted redbuds, planetary boxwood topiary, and a moody place to dine. My pea gravel and flagstone deck proved to be exactly the look and feel I wanted for my English Tudor home: organic, earthy, and aesthetically correct.

The approach to an entrance is the degree of pleasant anticipation, mystery, and curiosity we experience wondering what lies just beyond the entry. By virtue of the entry's role as a transition point, we experience the allure of the momentary unknown until we pass through the gate or fence, up the stairs, along the path, between the posts, or under the archway to discover the secrets and garden treasure that lie just beyond the threshold of the entry we have created. Flanking the walkway or porch steps with symmetrical interest of seasonal color, pots, or plantings conveys a sense of welcome and leads the eye to the entry itself. Entrances need not be abrupt. We can invite visitors to linger a bit, smell the fragrant plantings, and appreciate the sensory experience that's been created for them as they saunter to the ingress point. What we want to create is a delicious tease as to what other delicacies lie ahead. Such is the importance of the entry as a part of each garden room and outdoor space, no matter the style or aesthetic of the home and garden. Think of entry as an experience, a verb and activity, rather than just a fixed passage from one place to another.

Top: My friend Marquette has the cutest bungalow, complete with an appletini green door. It welcomes visitors up a stone walkway, through a white picket fence entry, and up the steps to the front porch.

Bottom: A side entry off the drive entices visitors to sit on the glider bench, which simultaneously serves as a retro focal point perfect for this spot.

My Theory of Garden Relativity

Each and every element in the garden relates to each and every other element in the garden for a cohesive, harmonious, rhythmic look and feel. (See page 87.)

Favorite Fragrant Rose Climbers and Ramblers for Arbors and Pergolas

- Yellow: 'Graham Thomas', 'Malvern Hills', 'Teasing Georgia'
- Pink: 'Gertrude Jekyll', 'Constance Spry'
- Apricot: 'Lady of Shalott', 'Crown Princess Margareta', 'Heritage'
- White: 'Snow Goose', 'Claire Austin'
- Magenta Pink: 'Tess of the d'Urbervilles'
- Red: 'Red Eden Climber'

A garden entrance is a great opportunity to create a beautiful first impression. It should reflect the style and architecture of the garden and home to make visual sense and create oneness with the landscape. An old, weathered gate at the entrance to my potager is decorated here for the season with sunflowers and a welcoming plaque.

The Fundamentals of Entry

A well-considered entry conveys importance to the space and to the garden visitor.

- A beautiful entry should be consistent in style with the garden, as a whole.
- A handsome entry is an opportunity to make a good first impression of that garden space.
- Entries can be grand or modest in nature, befitting the garden style and the personality of the gardener.
- Effective entry points might include an arbor, pergola, posts or pillars, gates, fences, hedging, containers, steps or a change in grade, or any combination of these.
- An entry sets the tone, mood, or role of a garden room or space.
- The most effective entries are experiential in nature, interactive, and participatory.

FRAMING THE VIEW

It's an easy thing to transition from the Entry design principle to another, Framing the View, because they so often work in tandem. The posts that constitute the entry into my kitchen garden not only welcome entrants, but also beautifully and symmetrically frame the view of the boxwood and

the secondary arbor that mirrors the entrance.

Consider framing the view as just that—placing or creating a frame of some sort around a beautifully composed picture, garden vignette, or spectacle. Framing the view elevates and enhances the beauty and importance of whatever it surrounds by focusing our gaze through the framework to what lies beyond. This could be from inside out to the

Above: Note the difference between the same roses here and on the opposite page. A completely different effect is created when the canes are not arched and distanced from the top of the fence; they just crawl along the pickets. Both are beautiful results, but in different ways.

Opposite: The arch of a climbing rose, carefully trained, creates a living window into the potager beyond

garden, from your bedroom or living room window, for example, or within the garden itself. The palladium window in my kitchen overlooking the backyard frames the view to the expanse of lawn and a large Chinese snowball *(Viburnum macrocephalum)* in the distance. A carefully pruned cascading limb of a redbud tree frames the view of the plants that fall within its contours. As I look out the window of where I now sit writing, its casing and outlines ever so effectively frame the most magnificent of borrowed landscapes—the snow-capped peaks of the great Rocky Mountains. Spectacle indeed!

An effective framed view may be symmetrical or more casual and asymmetrical, but it will always have a degree of equilibrium and balance—visual weight on each side of the frame that makes sense to the eye in a pleasing way. We often tend to think of long and elegant sight lines when considering this principle—on a long axis that may extend through multiple spaces into the vast beyond. But humble gardens on a much smaller scale can use the essence of this idea to heighten the experience of seeing the garden in varied and wonderful ways, adding layers of interest, personality, and a helpful lens for others to view our gardens in the appealing ways we see them.

Though partially hidden by vigorous hydrangeas *(Hydrangea macrophylla)*, nandina *(Nandina domestica)*, and larkspur *(Delphinium)*, this garden bench nevertheless captures the eye as a focal point amongst all the greenery and blooms.

The principle of framing the view does two things simultaneously to great effect: It circumscribes, enhances, and highlights the desired subject, putting it squarely within our line of vision, while also obscuring and screening out distractions that might diminish the beauty of what is being framed. As I write this, it occurs to me that each time I pick up my camera or shoot a video, I am doing the same. Trying to focus my vision on the beauty within the frame of the lens and removing the ugly or disorderly. To capture the towering dill, as it were, while hiding the ever-present garden hose. Really, designing our gardens in such a way as to frame the views we want to showcase is as simple as that. Showcasing the beautiful and editing out the rest.

The archway on my front side porch frames the view of the garden bed within its lines. A picket fence with side posts topped with finials frames the view into a vegetable garden. A carefully sculpted Japanese maple *(Acer palmatum)* delicately arching over a garden gate frames the view of what is in the distance. An allée of magnificent maples ablaze with autumn color frames the view to a home itself as one drives up the entrance. There are as many ways to frame a garden view as there are plants in the garden. Be creative and train your eye to frame the view of your surroundings in new and imaginative ways.

FOCAL POINT

Years ago, my husband and I made a pilgrimage to the land of the founding fathers and mothers of the United States. We visited Mount Vernon (home of George Washington), Highland (home of James Monroe), and Montpelier (home of James Madison). It was on this tour that I saw one of the best examples, and the absence of, the use of a focal point in all of my garden touring. Highland and Montpelier both have (I hope they *still* have them, given the presence of the dreaded boxwood blight appearing in that area) towering walls of American boxwood (*Buxus sempervirens*) on axis into other areas of the

landscape. At the apex of one, perfectly placed in the long sight line of those in the boxwood passage, was a beautifully positioned stone sculpture. At the apex of the other? Nothing. A visual disappointment despite the grandeur of the surrounding property. Such is the power of a focal point—that visual treat of something placed just so—that captures our attention, draws our eye and admiration, and punctuates and rewards our gaze and line of sight.

Some focal points are permanent and enduring, either by virtue of their weight, character, or expense if nothing else. Others can be dynamic, seasonal, and subject to the whims of the gardener. At varying times during the evolution of my own kitchen garden, the focal point holding center stage in the boxwood circle in the center of the potager has changed character dramatically. At differing stages in its maturity, it has held a scarecrow, bamboo teepee of climbing 'Wee Be Little' pumpkins, towering alliums, masses of tulips, container-grown olive trees, a weeping pussy willow, and now a simple but elegant olive urn. All were befitting the style of my garden, but ever so different in the tone, degree of sophistication, and type of materials they adopted.

The transformative power of the presence or absence of a focal point is immense. An area once considered less than special can be completely changed and elevated in stature with the addition of a perfectly staged focal point. Think of a stately, healthy tree of any kind in your backyard. Now, underneath the protective canopy of its foliage, imagine a bench with steppingstones leading to its promise of respite. Now mentally take that bench away as you gaze out your kitchen window. Do you miss it? Do you miss the story its presence told you? Now, in the bench's absence, place a stone birdbath nestled in a carpet of blooming ground cover and surrounded by the pendulous blooms of a large oakleaf hydrangea (*Hydrangea quercifolia*). Are you charmed by the picture you've just painted and the focus of your attention on the birdbath and its bathers?

One of the most effective and loved focal points in my own garden stands in the corner of the cut

These chairs, in addition to being practical seating in the warm sun, create a focal point out my kitchen window. The seating, along with the topiary display and sculpted viburnum in the distance, create a focal point vignette and tell a story.

flower bed across from the potager. It's a beautiful, hand-carved wooden dovecote that draws the eye, and alternately birds and wasps, but regardless of the inhabitants, it always makes a dramatic statement. Sometimes I clothe it in the exquisitely beautiful 'Trionfo Violetto' pole beans (*Phaseolus vulgaris* 'Trionfo Violetto') with their lavender blooms and deep purple pods with 'Purple Ruffles' sweet basil (*Ocimum basilicum* 'Purple Ruffles') at the base. Sometimes I hang a blooming basket of annuals just below the house itself. In winter, it holds its own, statuesque and informally elegant, bare of anything clothing its verticality. It serves as a wonderful punctuation point at the end of the flower bed, as well as a point of reference that visually helps adorn and organize the area.

In my opinion, the best focal points not only cry out for our attention, but they also call us to a point of engagement and interaction. *Watch* the birds splash in the birdbath or eat at the feeder. *Listen* to the gentle trickling or the dramatic waterfall of a water feature. *Smell* the fragrant roses on the metal tuteurs. *Harvest* the apples growing on the espalier. *Sit* on the bench under your old redbud tree as your sons or daughters practice their favorite super-power moves—demanding our attention even more effectively than the best of garden focal points. And, yes, that was a wonderful focal point flashback!

The Fundamentals of Focal Points

- Focal points work as visual hooks to capture your attention.
- Focal points focus your eye to a point of reference within a defined space.
- The best focal points call for engagement as well as attention.
- Focal points serve as visual exclamation points and punctuate spaces and areas of the landscape.
- Focal points serve as a point of reference for other things in the garden.

STRUCTURE

Oh, to have a greenhouse--a garden structure I am currently lusting after big time! I imagine myself inside it, puttering with my topiaries when the weather is inclement, housing them when temperatures dip below freezing, and admiring the greenhouse as a key design anchor and linchpin in my gardenscape.

Outbuildings of any kind in a garden (with the exception of outhouses perhaps, though I *have* seen them styled with great charm in some historic gardens) make up your garden structures. Have you heard the expression "Let's go visit the hollyhocks?" No? More often, gazebos, arbors, pergolas, chicken coops, pool houses, guest quarters, he-sheds, she-sheds, loggias, doll houses, and tree houses get noticed. The list of garden structures goes on and on, limited only by one's imagination, space, and pocketbooks. My own 1932 home has a detached garage with servant's quarters. We enlarged this antiquated space using one bay of the garage to create an office and studio for my husband and me. Two sides of the structure enter the garden through French doors, creating an indoor/outdoor space that gets heavy use.

Structures like mine, and many of a more modest nature, play varying roles in the garden. Some are utilitarian, such as tool sheds, dog houses, raised beds, trash can corrals, and chicken coops. Structures may be freestanding or attached, such as window boxes, trellising, and pergolas. But no matter the character and role, structures of any kind provide opportunities for stylistic expression and garden beautification.

Buildings as structures anchor themselves to the garden and provide surfaces, walls, and large expanses of space to adorn. These walls and expanses serve to enclose a space, lend intimacy, and provide a large surface to grow fabulous climbers or hang garden sculpture. Even common storage units found at almost any home improvement store can be elevated to the uncommon and quaint by hanging an awning over the doorway, installing a knocker or plaque on the door itself, and positioning two large pots with interesting plantings on either side. I recently heard the expression "romancing the common," and this kind of treatment does just that. Ornamental garden touches can make all the difference in transforming an overlooked garden component of any size or scale into something special.

Whether bland or grand, garden structures contribute to what we often call "good garden bones." Along with other good garden bones, such as large specimen trees and evergreen plantings, structures can be softened with looser and less architectural components—think blousy and billowy growers that relax the strict linearity of their geometric nature. When designed to match the style and concept of the landscape, garden structures contribute not only function and form, but they also bring cohesion and continuity to the landscape by visually uniting different areas. The arbors in my potager, detached and away from my home, as well as the window boxes that adorn the windows on the house itself, are stained to match the color of the trim on my home. This continuity of color and material helps all partners in the design dialogue of my garden speak the same language.

The Power of Three

It's a fairly well-known design principle that inside the home or out, the Rule of Three can create brilliant visual appeal and balance. Arranging pots, plants, or garden ornaments in odd numbers starting with three is more visually appealing, statement-making, and memorable than those arranged in even numbers. Except of course when perfect mirrored symmetry is the goal.

The same consistent vernacular and stylistic harmony concerns hold true for freestanding structures, such as tuteurs, trellises, arbors, and outdoor furniture. As Bunny Mellon, the famous tastemaker who designed the White House Rose Garden for John F. Kennedy once famously said, "Nothing should be noticed." Eye catching, yes, but slap-you-in-the-face contrast with the style of the home and garden, no. Gardening flourishes and ornaments should strive for the same beautiful compatibility with the surrounding garden as the structures themselves.

Container plantings in your landscape creates just the opportunity to put this power into practice. Three identical pots with identical plantings running up and down the back doorsteps create wonderful rhythm and harmony. Three pots of different sizes in scale to the setting can give perfect visual weight to a porch corner or effectively separate one garden room from another.

Need to break up a long, blank expanse of fence or wall? Consider positioning three tall evergreens—perhaps hollies *(Ilex)* or arborvitae *(Thuja)* with two on either end and one in the middle. If the expanse is too long even for this trio, then add two more positioned equidistant in the middle of these. Voila! You now have good structure on this once empty facade with room to play and compliments of the power of three or a version of it.

The Fundamentals of Structures

- Structures provide a permanent grounding element to the landscape.
- Structures provide a canvas for creative expression with plants and garden ornament.
- Structures should be harmonious in style with the garden itself and other structures.
- Structures may be utilitarian or aesthetic in nature.
- Structures can contribute a sense of privacy and enclosure in the garden.

COLOR

How many of us have been wooed into gardening by that great seductress of gardening, *color*? I know I was. It's hard to resist pulling out your credit card on a beautiful spring day when what seems like acres of colorful annuals and perennials lie before you in all their rainbow glory. Early on in my gardening career, I would inevitably go home with a bit of this color and a bit of that color because it was so hard to choose which hue I found most compelling.

Though difficult, having a more disciplined approach toward the use of color in your garden design will pay off immensely in both garden sophistication and satisfaction. In fact, though color enticed me into gardening, it is not what keeps me digging and planting. Now I find texture, shape, line, and form more of a priority than color, which tends to be more transitory and demanding to maintain over the seasons. Consequently, I think carefully about what mood and tone I want to create before making my seasonal color selections. A soft pastel English garden palette of lavender, white, pink, and yellow creates quite a different feel than a hot and fiery color blast of deep red, oranges, golds, and purples. The first lends itself to misty, soft light and generally cooler conditions. In hot climes, intense and vivid hues stand up to strong sun and washed-out light under a blazing sky.

What influences our color choices? Personal preferences, of course. Also, our climate, season, and geography. And last but not least, what colors and tones play well with the colors, tones, and architecture of your home. Remember, everything in our gardens relates to every other thing in our gardens, including color.

One of my favorite ways to play and design with color is to establish beautiful echoes based on common color characteristics between plants and even between different plants' various stages of growth. Blooms whose color perfectly matches the beautiful veining of another plant's foliage, or its stems and branches or buds and seed heads, is sophisticated and subtle yet highly impactful.

Above: This herringbone brick 'throw rug' I laid to replace the struggling ground cover is far more appealing and proved a great solution to a problem area.

Opposite: Color need not come from flowers or fruit alone! More and more exquisite plants are being bred for foliage color along with their blooms. These purple companions look elegant, complex, and colorful in a sophisticated way.

The Fundamentals of Color

- Color choices dictate mood and tone.
- Large swaths of color are more effective and visually travel greater distances than small patches of color.
- Color choices should be informed by the house and other surrounding elements.
- Color is not limited to flowers. Try infusing color using foliage, fruits and seed pods, branches, and edibles.
- Color is affected by the quality of light and the time of day and season.
- Plan your garden color around the seasons during which you enjoy the garden the most.
- Color = Work + Resources (labor, water, fertilizer, planting).

TEXTURE, PATTERN, RHYTHM, AND REPETITION

As much as I love color in the garden, it is now second in my affections to texture and textural contrasts when selecting plants. Surprises and fresh ways to combine textures, patterns, and leaf forms are all around us.

We humans are hard-wired to look for patterns in things; maybe that's why we find patterns and flow in the garden so pleasing and comforting: the pattern of the pickets on a picket fence, the lattice back of a chair, the bark on a tree, or black dots on a ladybug. Nature inspires us with its endless examples of patterns and rhythmic repeats that we can copy in our plantings and use of garden ornaments.

Nothing is more beautiful to me than the rhythm and repetition of a design element across a space—the pattern of urns running up and down a stone wall; a series of wooden tuteurs in the potager; an allée of apple trees leading up a drive or walkway. It is my favorite garden design principle and one that I take great joy and satisfaction in executing. In my front garden beds, I have a series of boxwood spheres that are planted rhythmically, if not perfectly equidistant, running through the beds. They have a soothing cadence about them as the movement of their placement draws your eye along the soft curves of the bed lines.

When I found it impossible to grow a consistently good-looking patch of ground cover in front of a garden bench under my redbud tree, I turned to brick in a herringbone pattern as an alternative. Easy care, good looking, and ever so functional with beautiful texture and rich organic color, it proved to be the perfect example of using texture, pattern, rhythm, and repetition to solve a vexing garden problem.

How you organize, access, and size your kitchen garden is a highly personalized thing. My friend Camilla did it her way, and appropriately so!

Chapter 4

GARDEN ORGANIZATION, SCALE, AND ACCESS

MAKE IT WORK

I just read an article from the January issue of a popular magazine with predictable resolution tips on getting your closets organized for the new year. It emphasized the importance of first culling out what you *don't* want/need or can't fit into, before heading to the container store for boxes and bins and bags to organize that closet, pantry, or drawer. You need to know the *size* of the contents before you can figure out the size of the *container* for the contents. I get it. This also happens to be good advice when establishing a plan and organizational strategy for starting a kitchen garden. The ambitions I had for my own potager initially were humble—some greens, herbs, and a few vegetables livened with a few blooms. I wanted something fresh to harvest daily, throughout all four seasons if possible. To a great extent, this remains true today, restricted as I am by the amount of space I tend. What I wanted to grow—i.e., the *contents* of my garden, dictated the size of the *container* for the contents—depended on the size, shape, and details of my potager.

Above and Left: My friend Laura converted a section of her driveway into a vegetable garden with raised beds and basket containers to match her Victorian-style home and an espalier to adorn her fence. An avid gardener, she knew what she wanted and set out to make it happen in a tidy, orderly way.

Opposite: What this home gardener can't squeeze into her raised beds gets planted in a series of matching pots along the fence. This gives her the option to plant or not to plant these good-looking containers that are handsome with or without inhabitants.

The layout, dedication of space, and parameters of your kitchen garden will be dictated and driven by these same considerations, the list of edibles and ornamentals you want to grow, the space you have, and the amount of time you can dedicate to its cultivation and success. In the headiness of spring with its cool temperatures, still-healthy plants, and reliable rainfall, it is easy to be overly ambitious with a "your eyes are too big for your stomach" mentality, especially if you have lots of room to indulge your gardening appetite. We have all seen gardens enthusiastically and naively started in spring only to be abandoned to heat, weeds, mosquitoes, and squash bugs in later summer, if not sooner. So, might I suggest the first place to start is with a good old reality check?

Secondly, I might humbly recommend that you refer to the list of questions that I posed in earlier chapters and how you answered them. Remember, everything in the garden relates in some way to every other thing, so consider the challenges of the site, what you like to eat, how much room and space it will require, and how the style of your garden fits into the overall landscape and its environment.

Of course, if you live on a small lot like mine, or you can only garden in containers like my sons, then decision making is that much easier as your options are limited. Nevertheless, no matter the size and scale of your garden, using common sense at the outset of the gardening season will prevent a bonanza of frustrations down the line. So, start with a checklist of considerations for the organization, scale, and garden access before moving forward.

VANTAGE POINT AND LOCATION

Wouldn't it be nice to have your kitchen garden, herb garden, or even your wine barrel planters just outside your kitchen or mudroom door? Maybe yes, and maybe no, depending on what your priorities are when it comes to maintenance, appearance, convenience, and the opportunity costs of having it close versus at a distance. On a cold, late fall morning, it might be nice to have that sage and those other sun-loving herbs and vegetables right outside your kitchen door for that roasting turkey. But, depending on your climate, that might mean your view is primarily empty vegetable and herb beds right outside your door and kitchen window as well.

Outside my own kitchen window, I prefer to look at the birdbath nestled in the shade-loving shrubs growing beneath a beautifully pruned redbud tree I raised from a seed that had planted itself there—too shady for sun-loving edibles, but perfect for viewing splashing birds out the French doors from my chair by the fireplace. Plus, a quiet, short stroll to the potager to clip my herbs is a welcome calm before the celebratory storm of cooking, feeding,

and entertaining. When I was unexpectedly laid up one summer, bedridden compliments of a sudden appendectomy, I was happy that my potager wasn't right out the window, taunting me with all the neglected to-dos and its untidy appearance. I liked that its ignored beds and pest-riddled foliage were hidden from my view, if not from my worries.

Of course, "hidden" can also be a way for you to ignore its maintenance and care. Out of sight, out of mind, as it were. Many gardens are consumed by weeds, bermudagrass, and pests because they aren't within easy viewing, at an easy reach, and in range of your guilty conscience. Know thyself as well as thy garden when considering its location.

Though my property is small, I am still fortunate to have a landscape large enough to make the location of my kitchen garden a choice rather than a dictated location due to a lack of real estate. Yet some of the most charming edible gardens I have seen have consumed no more than the length of a balcony railing and some strategically staged pots in a corner or in raised beds abutting the garage. No matter where you live, work with what you have, what you want, and what your kitchen garden needs to be successful.

Choosing a Good Site

Most vegetables need at least six hours of sun a day. Choose an open area with little to no shade. Here are other things to keep in mind when choosing a good site:

- Access to water is crucial. Watering cans, soaker hoses, in-ground irrigation systems, or sprinklers are all options.
- Good drainage is essential. Amend heavy clay or sandy soil with organic matter. Be aware that this will be a recurring practice as soil reverts to its original state and plants use and deplete nutrients and minerals as they grow.
- Protection from desiccating winds, hungry wildlife, and family pets should be considered. This could include the use of simple chicken wire cloches on one end of the extreme to fully enclosed dedicated garden spaces to keep out deer and other wildlife—or pets—on the other end of the spectrum.
- Good air circulation to prevent pest infestation and disease is important for healthy plants and a productive garden, not to mention a cool breeze and fewer mosquitoes for the working gardener.

This innovative planting tower serves as a high-rise condominium for herbs, cascading seasonal color, and small bushy peppers. When a gardener can't go out, a gardener goes up!

WHAT ABOUT A FRONT YARD LOCATION?

This option, along with religion, politics, and sex, is a controversial subject one must broach carefully, especially in the mixed company of neighbors, members of your homeowners' association, or in your gated community. If ever there was a reason to consider *Good Garden Fit* (see page 51) before taking on a gardening project, this would be that reason. The idealistic gardener in me is inclined to say, "YES! Go for it!" Especially if that is the only sunny spot you have to grow edibles. But the tidy pragmatist in me knows that gardening in a difficult zone where the best tended gardens, be they vegetable or ornamental, struggle to just remain *alive* by summer's end (and thus may be much less attractive). In some extreme cases, depending on where you live, a front yard garden might even be illegal.

It generally comes down to one or two issues: concerns over diminished property values and neighborhood landscaping norms, and the aesthetics of vegetables and vegetable gardening overall. So, check any zoning codes, HOA covenants, or neighborhood ordinances before building pricey raised beds or elaborate garden structures for your zucchini and indeterminate tomatoes. My neighborhood, in a historic preservation area, has certain regulations and building restrictions I must adhere to and be respectful of. Consequently, I must abide by them, try to remember the context of where I garden, be considerate of my neighbors and neighborhood, and try to garden responsibly, beautifully, and productively.

I am obsessed with this eco-friendly rooftop garden at Plenty Mercantile, a local business close to downtown Oklahoma City. It uses rain barrels to capture water, solar panels to capture sunlight, a pollinator garden to capture pollinators, and delicious veggies and a bar to capture clientele.

If you do decide on a front yard vegetable garden, do your homework. Locate examples in your own growing area that work both aesthetically and practically. Ask questions of your local horticultural extension centers, plant societies, and knowledgeable folk at farmers' markets and community supported agriculture groups (CSAs). Most importantly, dedicate and commit yourself to the project and the task. A front yard vegetable garden that is abandoned in mid-summer for lack of enthusiasm, effort, or skill can be disheartening to not only the homeowner but also to those living in the area. Also be mindful of what those beds will look like mid-winter, especially if you garden in areas with harsh winters and a limited growing season.

My happy compromise in my own front beds is edible landscaping—incorporating beautiful edibles into my gardens by using them for their ornamental value, rather than tearing up the front lawn for exclusive vegetable gardening and unnerving the neighbors. 'Purple Ruffles' basil will be as beautiful as any annual flower when planted next to orange cape honeysuckle (*Tecoma capensis*) with trailing purple scaevola and some bushy 'Patio Baby' eggplants. I can imagine completing this orange and purple vignette with gorgeous 'Trionfo Violetto' pole beans growing up the lamp post with perky orange marigolds or zinnias at the base. I doubt any neighbors would complain.

Claus Dalby, a famous Danish gardener, publisher, and photographer, is a master of container vegetable gardening. His coordinated use of containers—strategically limited in terms of variety, styles, and materials—gives this container garden a sense of cohesion and unity despite its complexity of plant material.

ROOFTOP VEGETABLE GARDENS

Nothing quite captures my imagination and fancy like the idea of a rooftop garden in the middle of a bustling urban center. Maybe it's the high-low tension of the city mouse and the country mouse having a meeting of the minds or too many rom-coms with a rooftop garden playing a major role. Nevertheless, there is no denying the charm, necessity, and possibilities of rooftop gardens. And if you garden for relaxation, for respite from life stressors, or as a mental health coping strategy, there is probably nowhere gardening is more imperative and valued than in the middle of a noisy, stress-filled city. Escaping to a rooftop garden to pluck some tomatoes and cut some blooms for your dinner table sounds like a wonderful version of living a garden lifestyle—all while overlooking the lights of the city at sunset.

Whether growing containers of herbs on a city fire escape or an entire green roof with soil and plants, rooftop gardens are gaining in popularity in both residential and commercial settings. It's not hard to see why. They put to use unused or underutilized space; allow for privacy; beautify a typically bland, ugly space; have good sun exposure; have no deer, rabbits, or voles; and most importantly, they can be very environmentally beneficial.

The scale and commitment of a rooftop garden varies from fully planted and cultivated green roofs, requiring input from structural engineers or architects (not to mention your landlord and building codes) to a few pots on a ledge. Most large rooftop gardens will understandably require more professional services and expense than deciding to start a vegetable garden in your backyard.

Container gardening is the easiest and most personal option for a rooftop garden. Growing a variety of container plants, hanging baskets, or raised beds gives the gardener the option of starting on a modest scale and growing the garden over time as interest, enthusiasm, and needs increase. Any style of gardening, from a mishmash of uncoordinated containers in all manner of materials to highly elegant stylized and customized planters constituting the look of a formal potager, can be realized—limited only by space, dreams, pocketbooks, and of course weight-bearing loads.

Rooftop container gardens are subject to the same care requirements and considerations of those on the ground, but with obvious additional issues and idiosyncrasies to be taken into account, do your homework beforehand.

SQUARE FOOT GARDENING

I love everything about the concept, design, and efficiency of square foot gardening. Square foot gardening is the practice of dividing a growing area, whether in the ground or in a raised bed, into small, usually one-foot (30 cm) square sections in a grid-like pattern. Typically, each square grows one featured type of vegetable, leafy green, or herb. The hope and objective are to simplify the planning, creation, production, and maintenance of a small but intensively planted vegetable garden.

Seeds or seedlings are planted in one or more squares based on plant size; for example, you would have more carrots per square foot (929 cm²), but only one tomato or bush bean. With no paths, there is no wasted space, the soil in the bed stays loose with no soil compaction caused by working gardeners, and the density of the plantings keeps weeding to a minimum. The plants themselves serve as living mulch, preventing weeds from germinating just as other traditional types of mulch do. This is my kind of an effective multitasker!

CONTAINER VEGETABLE GARDENING

For longer than I care to admit, I have done a weekly gardening segment on my local NBC affiliate television station. I still recall my very first topic and project, a container garden show-and-tell that I demonstrated in the studio. It was a huge container—a glazed blue pot—that I planted with all things related to making spaghetti sauce. It had a huge cherry tomato on a support in the center, along with bushy basils, garlic chives, cascading oregano, and parsley, and even some marigolds for a punch of color. It was beautiful if I do say so myself. Not long after I remember planting the same spaghetti-themed plants in huge empty tin cans of tomatoes and tomato sauce I procured from local Italian restaurants. These became give-away centerpieces for a fundraiser spaghetti dinner at my boys' elementary school. They were unique, fun, and inexpensive tin-can container plantings.

For the drama and novelty alone, I highly recommend vegetable gardening in pots—about as unfailing a method there is for dealing with problems related to weather, weed control, soil quality, and nibbling critters. Of course, there is also the obvious advantage that you do not need a large area or a dedicated in-ground patch to cultivate and grow edibles. Pots are great for urban gardeners, minimalist gardeners, or anyone interested in the tiny house craze! This spring, for weather- and time-related reasons, I never got around to planting my lettuce, arugula, and spinach in the potager beds. I was, however, able to plant several large pots of mesclun mix, microgreens, and delicate herbs in containers for my own nibbling needs. Small quantities, yes, but enough for healthy veggie wrap lunches, cilantro-topped tacos, and dinner side salads for my husband and me. Fresh daily, remember?

If you don't have room or time for a vegetable plot, then consider trying easy and fast-growing edibles in large containers. I emphasize *large* because small pots, which I consider to be anything under 12–16 inches (31–40 cm), will require constant tending and watering in the heat of the summer, sometimes as much as twice daily, depending on conditions. A larger volume of soil will hold nutrients and moisture for longer periods and give more leg room for healthy root growth. Obviously, another advantage to container gardening is portability.

Members of the nightshade family are among the easiest and I think most dramatic to grow in pots. Tomatoes, eggplant, potatoes, peppers, peas, lettuces, and other greens easily take to pot culture. Look for varieties that may be specifically labeled for patio pots or container culture. I find that as a rule, pretty much all dwarf varieties of veggies do well in containers, even those rampant vining ones such as squash and pumpkins. Try 'Honey Bear' acorn squash in a large pot, 'Jack Be Little' pumpkins, or 'Little Leaf' cucumbers. Staking and adding supports in some cases will be required, of course, but that is all part of the compositional creativity and fun related to gardening in pots. In my experience, this type of mini-gardening is especially fun for children or tiny-loving enthusiasts of any age. Space or time challenged? Consider a *potted potager* as an option.

I have long been fascinated by the concept of auricula and pelargonium theaters, a traditional way of displaying and showcasing these bloomers in a romantic, novel, and practical way. Details aside, the

This lush plant terrace is filled with potted chards, cabbages, and kales in the garden of Danish container master Claus Dalby. They look organized, well thought out, and uncluttered.

charm of this concept to me is to take one plant or type of plant and group them together in an attractive display. I love the repeated form of the same plant variety all lined up in similar containers on a terraced stage. I have done this in my own garden by creating a boxwood theatre, a myrtle topiary theatre, and a pelargonium and scented geranium theatre. I think some type of theatre dedicated specifically to edibles would be fabulous. If I had the room, I could imagine a fabulous display of just a few special herbs—maybe thymes, oreganos, and germanders. Can you imagine the fragrance, joy, and meditative calm of trimming, tending, and planting these edible summer stalwarts.

Tips for Starting Any Type of Edible Garden

If you are a beginning gardener, start small. As your enthusiasm, skills and motivation grows, you can always add to the garden space and the edibles you cultivate. At least at the outset, it's better to have a successful, well-tended small garden than a large one you can't keep up with, especially if you are just learning gardening fundamentals and are not sure if gardening as a hobby is right for you. Keep it simple, no larger than 10 × 10 feet (3 × 3 m) or even smaller or in containers. Select up to five types of vegetables, flowers, or some herbs to grow, and plant a few of each type. Do one thing at a time, do it well, then move on to and learn about the next thing.

INSPIRATION: SHAPE, DIMENSIONS, AND LAYOUT

Top: Humans aren't the only mammals we need to accommodate in our gardens. What about our trusty sidekicks?

Bottom: MY BAD! One of the biggest mistakes I made in planning my own potager was not giving myself adequate room to navigate and work within the confines of the boxwood edged beds. As they grew in girth and height over time, what was once easy to reach from the sides and the interior is now less accessible.

As you design the outline and shape of the garden, look for inspiration all around you. In my own gardens, I referenced the oval arches and door frames of my home, mimicking these architectural curves in my bed lines and planting drifts. A contemporary-style home might call for crisp, clean, straight lines to repeat the leading lines of the house or outbuilding. The height of a deck or other elevated structure might inform the height of a raised bed or a series of beds. These raised beds, though elevated, also can assume shapes, lines, and forms that are likewise inspired by architectural features.

The stone facade of a house might be the muse for a stone path, raised bed, or edging, which might hint at whether a formal or informal design is called for. Inspiration is all around us. But almost any pattern, formal or informal, is possible. Imaginative use of spirals, checkerboard designs, overlapping rectangles or circular, radiating beds are all possibilities. In my own potager, two stylized hearts face each other with a circle at the interface. Regardless of the shape, remember that as the garden and plantings mature, the outlines of the beds may blur. Vines may grow into paths, basil may spill over edging, and arugula may go to seed in the walkways and paths. Whenever possible, be generous with your measurements for paths and access avenues.

Raised beds, popular for their many advantages—both aesthetically and functionally—should have at least 2–5 feet (0.6–1.5 m) of path space between them, to accommodate you, your wheel-barrow, tiller, or other garden tools. If you have a loyal canine companion that accompanies you on your daily round, make sure to accommodate them as well.

Most raised beds range from 6–12 inches (15–31 cm) tall, with some as high as 36 inches (91 cm) and are garden structures, in their own right. Constructed out of brick, stone, stucco, wood, or metal, these impressive garden beds can brilliantly relate garden to home when speaking in the same tongue of design and material. But regardless of grandeur, size, or construction of the raised bed, it's still all about the growing medium itself for success and production. Generally, the poorer the quality of the underlying soil, the deeper the bed should be

to maximize the amount of good tilth available to plants. This provides more room and loose, friable soil for roots to grow and penetrate for moisture and nutrients.

As a rule, linear and raised beds are best kept to a maximum of four feet (1 m) wide. This allows the gardener to access the beds from both sides for weeding and harvest without stepping on and compacting the soil. Beds against a wall or fence should be about 2–3 feet (60–90 cm) wide as access for maintenance will only be from one side. As for the length or radius, consider how far and how many steps you want to get in before walking to the end of the space to tend the other side.

General Rules for Linear Beds

A north-south orientation is optimum for short crops, allowing sunlight to reach both sides of the bed. Taller plants should be planted to the north (I'm talking to you corn!), so as not to shade out shorter growing plants to the south (switch this orientation if you live in the southern hemisphere). Most vegetables should get six to eight hours of sunlight per day. Some greens, cool-season crops, and herbs can get by with as little as two to four hours, but sun and heat lovers, such as beans, tomatoes, peppers, and root crops, need more. But to every rule, there is an exception, and in the extreme heat of a southern summer, almost everything in the garden appreciates some afternoon shade.

Poor access planning on my part makes seeding, weeding, and harvesting in my potager difficult as the boxwood hedge has matured. As time passes, as I get older and my back hurts more, I have less tolerance for such things, and I am realizing that a change in design is an absolute necessity.

EDGING OPTIONS
FOR BEDS

LIVING EDGES AND HEDGES

When I first fell in love with the potager at Barnsley House in the Cotswolds, I was responding to the magical synergy of multiple things. The tidy geometry of the layout, the textures, the scents and beauty of the edibles, and the living, breathing aura of it all. But what struck me most was the fabulous way it was defined, circumscribed, and set off by the beautiful boxwood hedge surrounding the different planting zones. Thus, the inspirational seeds of my own boxwood-framed potager were planted. I knew the boxwood was crucial to the look and style I was trying to achieve.

Rosemary Verey's potager used Dwarf English boxwood, *Buxus sempervirens* 'Suffruticosa', *a* slow-growing variety once ideal for edging and borders. Sadly, it no longer can claim to be ideal. (For more information on boxwood blight and boxwood tree moth, consult the Plant and Pest Diagnostic Laboratory at Purdue University. www.ppdl.purdue.edu)

The scourge of boxwood blight has now travelled around the world, and though these issues have yet to appear in my own garden, their very existence would honestly have made me hesitant to use this favorite shrub of mine as the keystone planting of my kitchen garden. When I first planted my hedge almost thirty years ago, these two deadly forces were not an issue. Fortunately, I planted one of the more resistant varieties, a Korean boxwood, *Buxus sinica* var. *insularis* 'Wintergreen', formerly known as *Buxus microphylla* var. *koreana*, because of its bright green foliage, receptivity to frequent tight clipping, and lower cost relative to other varieties. In hindsight, in addition to these pest and disease concerns, I would have chosen a variety that did not grow so quickly and require such frequent pruning to keep it in tight and tidy form. Either of my current favorite boxwood varieties, 'Green Mountain' or Baby Gem™, would be slower growing, equally as beautiful, and not as high maintenance.

If I lived in a more temperate climate, I would consider rosemary, lavender, or santolina as a hedge alternative. Wall germander *(Teucrium chamaedrys)* is also of increasing interest to me, for its lovely scent, bee-attracting prowess, and dark green foliage.

NATURAL, ORGANIC BORDERS

Borders made of organic materials, whether for raised beds or at ground level, are beautiful and sustainable options, especially when repeating hardscaping materials already used in the home and surrounding areas. Think untreated wood, stone, brick, distressed metal, wattle, cement pavers, or even shells. Nothing will convey the style of your garden quite as emphatically as the materials you use to surround and edge your beds.

PATHS AND GARDEN FLOORING

The longer I garden, the more obsessed I become with the "floors" of garden spaces, both from a practical standpoint and an aesthetic one. When I first started my backyard garden, we did what most people did then. We built a wooden redwood deck off our back door laundry and kitchen area. It was expensive to build in both material and labor even then and would be even more expensive now. At the time I was thrilled with it, and my family of two young boys plus my husband and I used it extensively.

We put the requisite outdoor table and umbrella in place, and as my gardening became more feverish, I added more and more topiary and pots to add greenery and enclose the dining space.

Meanwhile, I kept reading and learning more and more about English gardening, the style of my English Tudor home, and the language of materials used to speak its architecture. As time passed, the deck inevitably aged, nails started to erupt from the planks, and even that natural wood surface burned the bare feet of my small boys when temperatures soared. And no matter how hard I tried, I just couldn't seem to soften its edges appropriately. It always looked out of place and out of character where the wood deck met up against the brick

This beautiful garden at Bustani Plant Farm in Stillwater, Oklahoma, has doubled up on its organic borders. The beautiful hand-constructed wattle fence is outlined with wood framing and generous gravel paths. Thanks to my friends Steve and Ruth Owens at Bustani Plant Farm in Stillwater, Oklahoma, for the image of this wattle fence and generous gravel paths.

walls of my home. Eventually, it began to look more "suburbia" to me than English Tudor in style and even in functionality. Still, it served us well and we used it until it needed replacing many years later.

Replacing it with what I had in mind was a big risk for this self-taught gardener and garden designer. I really didn't know what I was doing, but I did know certain things that drove my vision.

1. I wanted it to look more consonant with my English Tudor home.
2. I wanted to use only the hardscape materials that already existed in its facade.
3. I wanted it to look consistent with a true English garden, not just consistent with the architecture of my home.
4. I didn't want the upkeep and initial expense of another redwood deck.
5. I wanted a more spacious open feel that flowed more easily into the grade of the grassy turf and could then flow and be incorporated into the paths of the potager.

I took this list of wants to the company who executed the design, and we came up with a plan and a sketch. Nothing complex, but innovative I think for the time. They constructed a set of wide stone steps with a large launch and landing pad right outside the back door. This spacious step needed to be large enough to accommodate the firewood holder for the kitchen fireplace in the winter and my terraced plant stand for my topiary in the summer. I wanted the risers to be shallow for easier access for aging friends and relatives, and wide enough for more large, potted evergreens. We fashioned the steps out of flagstone that matched the stone on my house and half-brick risers to match the brick on my house.

These wide, slow steps led to a deck and dining area now made out of large pieces of flagstone in designated path areas leading to driveway gates, and in areas where the outdoor dining furniture would be placed.

It was all graded and leveled before a base of crushed gravel was put down underneath a layer of natural colored pea gravel that coordinated with

the color of the flagstone. Finally, I had the English garden look and feel I had been envisioning. I later added some aged brick around the perimeter of the space and throughout the garden. Flagstone pavers embedded in the turf lead to the entrance to the potager, where paths of like materials, flagstone, gravel, and brick make up the walkways and access points.

Even in the winter, the gravel deck with the brick and flagstone edging softens the look of the space and echoes the curves and lines of the arches and windows on my house.

Consequently, the flow of "flooring" materials from the house to the deck and ultimately to the lawn, garden rooms, and the potager remained the same, consistent in materials, look, and language. Regardless of the materials and stylistic language your home and garden speak, the same overarching considerations should be considered to achieve seamless, harmonious elegance.

> "IT IS NOT THE STRONGEST OF THE SPECIES THAT
> SURVIVES, NOR THE MOST INTELLIGENT THAT SURVIVES.
> IT IS THE ONE THAT IS MOST ADAPTABLE TO CHANGE."
> —LEON C. MEGGINSON (1921–2010)

Chapter 5

FLEXIBILITY AND ADAPTABILITY

THINK BOTH SHORT AND LONG TERM

As families grow, as gardeners age, or as interests change, gardens must adapt to meet the needs of the gardeners. This keeps gardens and gardeners fresh and continually excited and open to new and beautiful possibilities for the future. Over the years, I've helped a number of families downsize or upsize their gardens, depending on their stage of life and the demands of their children, their health, their time, and, yes, their pets. One of the most beautiful, unique, and Pinterest-pinned kitchen gardens I have ever encountered was built in a terraced fashion, planted in a gorgeous combination of flowers, herbs, and vegetables—and then later removed by its owner to make room for a dog run.

While it may not have been the change I would have made, she nevertheless adapted in a very personal way her kitchen garden to meet her own individual priorities and interests. She now gardens in containers and her dog has room to roam.

A young gardening friend of mine who discovered gardening to her great delight during the pandemic shutdown started with a few herbs and vegetables planted in a narrow west-facing strip of earth abutting her fence. She slowly added container after container of more herbs and veggies as her passion grew. She purchased a new house recently and is analyzing how she wants to make space for her new obsession and is looking at various options. In the process, she has been like a sponge, asking advice, opinions, and garnering wisdom from anyone and everyone in her orbit who gardens. Smart girl. Nothing is wiser than flattening your own learning

Left: This elegant terraced potager designed by my friend and landscape architect John Fluitt is on my own inspiration board for my future garden self.

Most gardeners are generous with their knowledge and will happily share their winners and losers when it comes to specific varieties, composting techniques, favorite garden tools, and best practices for your area and climate. It's a great opportunity for cross generational relationships to begin and have a lot of fun in the process.

curve by mining information, sharing trial and error experiences, and getting specific information about your particular growing zone from and with others.

I continually make small changes to modify my own garden and am constantly looking for ways to make it adapt to my own changing priorities, needs, wants, and physical constraints. I think one of the biggest mistakes we can make down the line—after we have gardened in a certain space and in a certain way—is to fail to acknowledge the *need for change*. It is sometimes hard to scrutinize a garden that we have had for years, and tended in the same way for years, to recognize that a change is in order. We need to continually analyze what is still working and what doesn't work any longer. Recognizing a need for change is hard.

I helped my friend Elaine design this small kitchen garden over fifteen years ago. When it was time for a change, a new more user-friendly design with a different aesthetic was executed to meet her current needs. The new design has a more modern, updated look that still matches the style of her home. See the new garden on page 82.

Executing and implementing those changes is even harder. But I think doing so is crucial to our continued enjoyment of gardening itself. We may be in denial over our aging selves and the need for change. We may be hesitant to alter a much-loved design that has overgrown its stay. Or it may just be the sheer centrifugal force of keeping things as they are. However, the expression "Use the right tool for the job in the right way" applies here. Using the right tool for a job makes the work more pleasurable, productive, and efficient. The same can be said for a garden that fits the demands, job requirements, and needs of the gardener.

Our ultimate garden goal should always be to think of our garden as a gift, not a burden. If we don't make necessary changes, what was once our delight can become our dread. Of course, goals are not reality, but are just that, goals. Something we are always pursuing, but never entirely reach to perfection. It is a practice, not a destination. Our own personal garden pilgrimages as we cultivate our bits of earth over the years.

My husband owns a business that designs and outfits commercial office space with furniture, office storage, and modular walls and panels. These moveable fixtures make enlarging, modifying, and reducing individual office spaces easy, customizable, cost effective, and very adaptable to dynamic businesses and changing business needs. More importantly, his designs are effective, personal, problem solving, and can be quite beautiful. These are all qualities that I find valuable in creating modern, elegant kitchen gardens and potagers of any size or scale. Like these businesses, we gardeners as "clients" should demand the same flexibility, long-term strategizing, customization, and adaptability of our own garden designs—both in how we create them and what we grow in them.

As young families grow, an expansion of a vegetable garden and its growing space might

become a priority. With more mouths to feed and more healthy eating lessons to teach, this might seem obvious. But not necessarily so. I am one of ten children, but growing up, with the exception of a few tomatoes and some herbs, we did not have a seasonal vegetable garden that we tended each growing season despite the large number of those mouths to feed and a readily available child labor pool for weeding, planting, and harvesting (trust me, that built-in labor pool labored on other things, I assure you). It wasn't for lack of space—we lived in suburbia with a large yard and lots of growing room that could expand at whim. Rather, it was for lack of time to plan, other life priorities (just day-to-day survival!), and the vegetables-come-out-of-a-can mentality of that decade and its obsession with convenience, frozen foods, and supermarkets.

Ironically, it was only *after* most of us had grown up and flown the coop that my parents decided to cultivate and tend a rather large, in-ground vegetable garden on a lot they purchased next

to our home. It was filled with Indiana sweet corn, green beans, lots of tomatoes, herbs, and other delectables. More free time and their retirement made such a garden possible for them, along with continued good health, reliable Indiana rainfall, a good tiller, and lots of neighbors and friends happy to share in the excess. And those now adult children who would come home to help. At the time, raised beds had not reached the popularity they enjoy today. So, when they were ready to downsize their in-ground vegetable garden, no structural changes or bed removals were necessary. They simply sold the lot to some good friends of theirs who built a home in its place, and my mother created a small herb garden with a few tomato plants behind the house. I don't know that they planned any of those design changes at the outset of starting the garden, but it certainly worked out in elegant fashion for them in the end.

Opposite: When the twenty-year old arbor at the entrance to the potager needed to be replaced, an alternative entry was designed instead. A change that opened up the garden and gave it a fresh look and feel.

Above: This ready-made, raised bed kit from Gardener's Supply is easy to put together and stylish. Copper post caps elevate the look.

RAISED BED GARDENS

Raised bed gardens epitomize flexibility in creating and modifying kitchen gardens. Ready-made kits made from both wood and metal are easy to find and construct and can be made to custom fit your growing location. Obviously, more permanent raised beds constructed to remain in place over time are not so changeable, so the type of raised bed gardening you do might be influenced by this consideration at the outset. Inexpensive kits available online and at your local home improvement store, to metal-frame, customizable panels in a variety of depths, colors, and detailing to fit your aesthetic style are all available. Researching options, costs, and different looks and reading reviews from other gardeners will help you make selections that are

right for you. Relatively quick and easy to install, add to, and take down, such flexible garden bed options might be just right for you. Just keep in mind all the factors mentioned on page 108 when selecting your site, keeping in mind first and foremost what you want to grow and eat. If upfront expense is an issue, I suggest you add modules over time, request them as gifts for birthdays and holidays, and watch for sales at the beginning and end of the gardening season.

No garden is without problems. As mine has aged, the boxwood has grown much larger than is shown in this photo. It is now so wide, it has reduced the amount of room I have to grow.

MY POTAGER THROUGH TIME

When I first designed my box-edged potager, I admit to giving little thought to how it would expand, contract, or change over time to meet my changing needs. My priority was first beauty and creating a certain aesthetic, and secondly to address the cultivation needs of my plants and what I wanted to grow. It was only as the potager evolved over time, and I recognized the shortcomings and practical design flaws of the area, that I began to think about ways to modify the space for better functionality, increased productivity, and in a manner that wouldn't sacrifice or change the essence of my original concept. Here are some of the options I am considering to change the design of my own overgrown hedged potager to address problems and issues that have developed as the garden has matured and to meet my own changing tastes and style preferences.

PROBLEM 1:
OVERGROWN BOXWOOD HEDGE SIDES

Each side section of boxwood hedge has ultimately grown too wide and is reducing the amount of space in each quadrant for growing herbs and vegetables.

Possible Solutions

I. Do a hard and major prune in late winter/early spring to reduce the height and width of the hedge. Things to consider: Timing and weather would be crucial. Optimally, this should be done just as winter heads into spring and the boxwood is starting to put out aggressive new growth. Hedge would look woody and bare during recovery and regrowth. Recovery and regrowth could be uneven over all four sections and lack symmetry. Some degree of risk involved. Process would take time, and I might lose a season of beauty.

II. Allow the hedge to keep growing in width and leave only enough space in the interior for singular large container plantings of herbs and vegetables.

Things to consider: More thinning and less shearing when pruning would be needed to keep it healthy and thick, and more pruning overall would be involved. All four access points would need to be improved and expanded.

III. Completely remove side hedge sections and replace with wattle or a natural material flexible edging in the same curved manner. Things to consider: No rubber or plastic material is an option. Soft-set brick or stone would be an initial expense in labor and materials and could also be dislodged if soft set. Boxwood balls and the interior circle of boxwood would remain.

PROBLEM 2: OVERGROWN STATEMENT BOXWOOD BALLS

Overgrown statement boxwood balls at the garden's east and west ends impede access for planting and pruning.

Possible Solutions

I. Reduce size of balls with a hard prune in late winter/early spring to reduce overall size by half. Things to consider: Should not be done all at once. Would take multiple seasons and some degree of risk involved based on weather and timing. Side hedges could remain or be removed.

II. Remove boxwood balls completely and transplant elsewhere. Things to consider: Location for transplants. Would remove a key design feature that is one of my favorite things about the space. Some degree of risk. Side hedges would remain.

PROBLEM 3: CONSTANT PRUNING AND MAINTENANCE OF BOXWOOD HEDGE

The work involved to properly prune and maintain the boxwood hedge is becoming increasingly time consuming and more tedious as I age. Fear of devastating insect and disease pathogens, such as boxwood blight and caterpillar moth, increase anxiety and could lay waste to the entire design.

Possible Solutions

I. Remove entire boxwood potager hedge and replace with low-maintenance raised beds customized to fit the space and that would be appropriate to my overall English garden design. Retain some of the boxwood for punctuation points of new raised beds to unify the potager with other areas of the garden containing box wood. Things to consider: Emotional upheaval of removing a much-loved, signature feature of my garden. Initial expense of labor and materials related to the new design. Decisions about materials to use, shape, and scale could be difficult. Major change is hard and disruptive.

As I work through the issues of adapting my own potager to my current life situation, I have empathy for anyone else doing the same. I have not yet decided on my final strategy, but thinking through my options over the past few years has helped me come to terms with what needs to be done, what will be involved, and the implications of the changes. It is easy to remove, replace, or change a feature of your garden that is dead, struggling, or unhealthy. I find it more difficult to modify and change or transplant a feature that is thriving.

The deep red veins of this 'Ruby Red' chard are an invitation for 'Profusion Red' zinnias (*Zinnia elegans* 'Profusion Red') and deep orange New Guinea impatiens (*Impatiens hawkeri*) to join the party.

WHAT TO GROW

Even the varieties and types of edibles you grow may change through the years. When my two boys were small, growing 'Wee Be Little' pumpkins on a bamboo pyramid in the center of the potager was fun, and we all garnered much delight and fun out of the process. But even this small display required much tending in the way of taming wild stems, warding off squash bugs, and keeping powdery mildew at bay. As these boys grew into hungry small men, the time and effort to grow those pumpkins was diverted to growing poblano peppers for stuffing and more basil for pesto making. Equally as beautiful and functional, but in entirely different ways. This proved to be a great example of *growing what you love to use and eat* (especially when garden space is limited) and *matching the demands of the garden to the demands of your life and appetites*. They were also easier to grow. In that vein, as I changed as well, I realized that I wanted a garden that was easier to maintain. Truly, a key consideration in selecting what you want to grow—both as edibles *and* as ornamentals.

If you dream of large watermelon patches, mounds of pumpkins for fall, and infinite bundles of asparagus in spring, then raised bed gardens won't be for you. What you want to grow will dictate to a great extent how you grow it. I am especially fond of dwarf and container culture varieties as they suit the space limitations of my small garden, and I find them cute—dollhouse cute. In this case, size matters but err toward the petite and diminutive. I talked about these tiny treasures in chapter 4, but it bears repeating: If you want to get a child interested in gardening, may I suggest starting with something cute? Like tiny eggplants and squashes or mini-sized lettuces and carrots? New cultivars are constantly being developed, so it is a fun category of edibles to explore. The graphic on the next page lists just a small sampling of the easy dwarf varieties of edibles to grow.

THE ULTIMATE ADAPTATION

There is one other option I have not yet addressed: deciding *not to decide*. Deciding not to decide is a decision itself, of course. I could do nothing to the design and let it be up to future owners of my home and gardens to decide on how they would choose to use and transform this space. What I once thought unthinkable—and many of my friends and followers still think it to be so—is now an option becoming more and more appealing to me. The idea of starting a whole new garden in a new place with new ideas and aesthetics is invigorating, intimidating, and tantalizing. It would be a way to reinvent my garden and my garden lifestyle in a whole new way—with new challenges and possibilities and new opportunities for growth and learning. This would be true whether the new garden was larger or smaller or in a different zone entirely. So, could I ever leave it? Yes. And *especially* in summer when temperatures soar and I begin to think of my garden as a burden, not a gift!

Strategies to Make Your Garden Easier to Maintain

- Replace perennial plants that have to be divided, deadheaded, and fertilized with blooming and fruiting small shrubs and trees—both evergreen and deciduous.
- Consider replacing high maintenance turf with a lower maintenance alternative: gravel, ground covers, flagstone, expanded garden beds, or high quality, highly realistic synthetic turf.
- Plant bushy varieties versus climbing varieties of edibles and flowers that require little to no staking or support.
- Plant intensely to avoid areas for weeds to set seed.

- Plant fewer seasonal annuals in large quantities in your garden beds. Concentrate color in pots and in punctuation points in your garden beds.
- Install an in-ground irrigation system at the root zone in your garden beds and use drip irrigation for containers and elevated beds. Mulch to prevent moisture loss.
- Don't let perfect be the enemy of the good. Remember that our gardens are living, breathing organisms just like us, imperfect and flawed.

Easy to Grow Dwarf Vegetables

'LITTLE LEAF' CUCUMBER
FRUIT 3–4" (8–10 CM) LONG, PRODUCE UNDER STRESS AND WITHOUT POLLINATORS

'POMEGRANATE CRUNCH'
MINI ROMAINE AND BUTTERHEAD CROSS, SMALL DENSE HEADS

'THUMBELINA' CARROT
GOLF BALL-SIZED CARROT, SOFT SKIN THAT DOESN'T HAVE TO BE PEELED

'EASTER EGG' EGGPLANT
EGG-SHAPED FRUIT THAT TURNS PASTEL COLORS, ORNAMENTAL

'MINNESOTA MIDGET' MELLON
SUPER SWEET FLAVOR, SIZE OF A SOFTBALL, DISEASE RESISTANT

'BABY BOO' PUMPKIN
GROWS TO 3" (8 CM) IN DIAMETER BY 2" (5 CM) TALL, ALL WHITE

Change the color palette of your garden by changing the things you grow. These blue podded peas put off a completely different vibe than would orange habanero peppers.

ADAPTIVE GARDENING

For years, I have done a gardening segment here in Oklahoma City on my local NBC affiliate station. For quite a few of those years, my friend Jim Miller, the Savvy Senior, did the same and we were on the same show. While waiting to go on, we would visit about a lot of things related to aging and very specifically about ways to adapt as one ages. Arthritis, back pain, risk of dehydration, and loss of strength and balance are all issues we begin to experience, and we must adapt to them as we age along with

our gardens. Our gardening capabilities change and are, in all likelihood, different in our thirties and forties than when we gardened in our twenties, and probably even more compromised in our seventies and eighties and even nineties.

Here are some tips Jim shared with me that can help all of us mitigate the effects of time and aging and help us garden for a lifetime. I have listed in the resource section some of the products and sources for items he recommends.

Tips and Tools for Older Gardeners

by Savvy Senior syndicated columnist and easier aging guru Jim Miller. Jim is a contributor to *HuffPost*, *KFOR-TV*, and *NBC Today*.

Warm Up

With gardening, good form is very important as well as not overdoing any one activity. A common problem is that gardeners often kneel or squat, putting extra pressure on their knees. Then, to spare their knees, they might stand and bend over for long stretches to weed, dig, and plant, straining their back and spine.

To help protect your body, you need to warm up before beginning. Start by stretching, focusing on the legs and lower back. And keep changing positions and activities.

Labor-Saving Tools

The right gardening equipment can help too. Kneeling pads can protect knees, and garden seats or stools are both back and knee savers. Lightweight garden carts can make hauling bags of mulch, dirt, plants, or other heavy objects much easier. And long-handled gardening tools can help ease the strain on the back by keeping you in a standing upright position versus bent over.

Easier Watering

The chore of carrying water or handling a heavy, awkward hose can also be difficult for older gardeners. Some helpful options include lightweight fabric hoses instead of heavy rubber hoses, soaker or drip hoses that can be snaked throughout the garden, thin coil hoses that can be used on the patio or small areas, a hose caddy and reel for easier hose transport around the yard, and a self-winding hose chest that puts the hose up automatically. There are also a variety of ergonomic watering wands that are lightweight, easy to grip, and reach those hard-to-get-to plants.

To find ergonomic gardening tools and the recommended watering aids, check with local retail stores that sell lawn and garden supplies. A recommended list of products and suppliers is in the resource section on page 198.

FUTURE INSPIRATION

However you hope to adapt and change your garden, on a large scale or a small one, stay organized and plan ahead. It's entertaining and creativity inducing to start and maintain an inspiration or mood board that channels the direction you hope to go. Whether it is digital on a social media platform like Instagram or Pinterest, Houzz, or a bulletin board with carefully curated ideas and images (my preferred method), you will find it very helpful and fun.

Left: The rich red of cherry tomatoes *(Solanum lycopersicum var. cerasiforme)* with a glossy coating of olive oil, waiting to be roasted then sprinkled with a chiffonade of basil is the color and essence of a summer garden.

Opposite: Nothing is more colorful or beautiful than a basket of freshly picked fruits, vegetables, and garden greens. No need for a centerpiece when what you serve is this strikingly beautiful. This image is one I captured during a *Victoria* magazine shoot.

Chapter 6

COLOR AND COMPOSITION

EXPRESS YOURSELF

This growing season, I have far more color in both my vegetable and ornamental garden beds than ever before. Thirty whole years of ever before. Why? Because I have more *sun* than I have had in years, compliments of an epic ice storm and a record-breaking arctic blast. The harsh winter weather felled shade-producing trees, brutally damaged those that remained standing, and killed understory plantings that protected and sheltered their underlings to a certain degree. Yes, history reminds me, there is a reason so few large trees grow on prairie soil. I have been known to say—not completely sarcastically—that in Oklahoma, even trees are annuals.

In past years, especially in the summer, my color palette spoke in a whisper. Colors were soft, largely pastel in hue, and accentuated the style and aura of my English Tudor architecture. Not so now, as I am planning a color combo far more flamboyant, loud, and befitting more and stronger sun and light—and rather uncharacteristically for me, I might add. If it doesn't scream, *"LOOK AT ME!"* this year, it will, at the very least, speak above a restrained whisper. Such is the power and emotion of color, in life and in the garden. Color has the ability to elevate, complement, or add to the impact of any garden design. It can also do the same to a person's mood and outlook on life itself. In a climate of relentlessly cloudy days, effective use of color can brighten up a garden bed and a person's attitude in the process.

Not even a spooky jack-o'-lantern could scare away an epic October ice storm that did heartbreaking damage to my 100-year-old oak *(Quercus)* and countless other stately trees throughout the city and state. Mother Nature forces change, whether we are prepared for it or not.

One thing I know for sure from my observations of other gardens, public spaces, and the gregarious colors of Disneyland, is that t*he fewer colors you combine and the more simplistic the design, the more calming it will feel.* In my opinion, it is also more beautiful and serene, regardless of whether those colors are loud and raucous or subdued and pastel. Lots of different colors might be invigorating and attention-grabbing, but they also can be disturbing and overstimulating. I find a restricted color palette to be far more sophisticated and elegant in appearance than one with a cacophony of color. You may disagree. Gardening is a very subjective combination of science and art, after all. Beauty truly does lie in the eye of the beholder. If your heart and soul need color, go for it, and pay no attention to this writer behind the curtain.

Today in gardens around the world, huge dramatic drifts of a single plant or plants in a restrained color scheme are gaining in popularity in both public and private landscapes. This prudent use of color is also effective in small gardens. In my view, the smaller the garden, the more restricted the range of colors if a cohesive, harmonious aura is to be achieved.

That said, here's a message to the color enthusiasts out there: It would be disingenuous for me to claim that successful, pleasing results can only be achieved by limited and restrained shades of color singing harmoniously in unison. Exuberant displays of bright, cheerful, sometimes overwhelming numbers of colors can be a delight in large public spaces with massive, complex, and flamboyant displays. But that same exuberance so impactful on a large scale might seem garish and overpowering in a small residential setting. Context, remember?

More than three colors (remember "The Power of Three" on page 99) can exhaust the eye and make it difficult to absorb the sense of the design. Keep it simple and elegant. Don't feel compelled to use every crayon in the box.

A striking, but restrained display at the Dallas Arboretum and Botanical Garden consists of broad sweeps of Intenz™ celosia (*Celosia argentea* 'Spitenz') in the foreground, with 'Fireworks' purple fountain grass (*Pennisetum setaceum* 'Fireworks') and 'Thai Black' banana (*Musa balbisiana* 'Thai Black') in the midspace and background.

Change to If you are trying to have a certain color or hue from the self-seeders in your garden, make sure to mark those you are selecting before the blooms fade and color can no longer be determined.

I mean, really? Is there anything cheerier than a red strawberry, ripened by the sun, with a green wannabe in waiting? I think not! This image reminds me of so many children's books I read to my boys when they were small.

THE COLOR WHEEL

First presented by Isaac Newton in 1666, the color wheel maps the color spectrum onto a circle, enabling us to see the relationship between colors. Analyzing and studying these relationships helps us create color harmonies and effective color combinations. But let's be honest. When was the last time you consulted a color wheel before planting your flower beds or before sowing seeds in your vegetable garden? Instead, I think we gardeners use the color wheel intuitively, based on our preferences for primary colors (colors that can't be mixed from other colors—red, yellow, and blue) or secondary colors (colors that result from mixing two primary colors, such as purple, orange, and green.) We design our gardens based on colors we like and dislike and migrate toward specific colors instinctively and viscerally. Or perhaps based on what looks especially tasty, fresh, and vibrant on the day we visit the nursery, farmers' market, or garden center!

The color wheel also can be divided into warm and cool colors, resulting in color temperatures. My home as it exists now is filled with warm colors—red through to yellow, but I notice as I get older, I am attracted more to cool colors—from blue to green to purple. This demonstrates that while we may have preferences for certain colors and hues, these preferences are dynamic and can change and evolve over time. Experimenting with different colors and color combos is a wonderful way to refresh the look of your gardens over seasons and years and express your changing personality and tastes. Like Picasso, you may find yourself experiencing a "blue" period in your garden one year and a "rose" period the next. Playing with color in the garden is one way to constantly nurture our youthful capacity for delight, discovery, and experimentation no matter what our age.

Opposite: Complementary colors at play in the flower border across from my potager. Texture + Color = Fabulous. It's basic gardening math.

Below: My favorite combos on the color wheel tend to be monochromatic and analogous. But to teach and humble me, Mother Nature often self-seeds bright, complementary colors together in the garden that are so exceptional it puts all my color planning to shame.

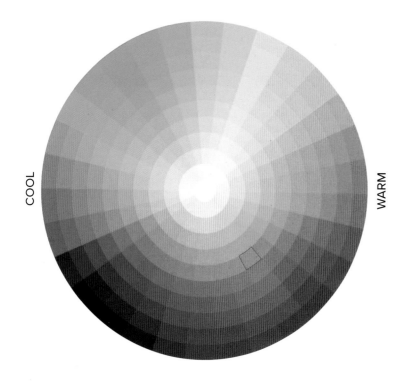

COOL   WARM

MONOCHROMATIC
COLORS OF SINGLE HUE

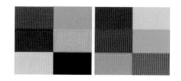

COMPLEMENTARY
COLORS OPPOSITE EACH OTHER
ON THE COLOR WHEEL

ANALOGOUS
COLORS THAT ARE ADJACENT TO EACH
OTHER ON THE COLOR WHEEL

COLOR PSYCHOLOGY AND OUR RELATIONSHIP TO IT

Common color psychology tells us that warm colors evoke energy and optimism and, in certain circumstances, even danger. Cool colors, on the other hand, can relax and soothe us, but they also can express melancholy and sadness. In selecting colors for my own landscape, considering the cultural needs of the plants, I can go in either direction when getting out my message. Warm colors can match the energy, heat intensity, and strong sun of a typical garden in the southern United States, or cool colors and tones can diffuse the heat and evoke the cooling effects of water or ice. Both are appropriate to a hot-as-the-dickens Oklahoma garden, depending on the effects I am trying to elicit.

But if I have learned anything about southern, hot weather gardening and the use of color in the summer months, it is that *more color = more work + resources*. Just like *color + texture = fabulous*. It's basic math. This irrefutable equation is even part of my personal "Garden Manifesto" (see page 59). Growing and planting color of *any* kind in *any* temperature in summers with extreme heat means more work and resources in the way of planting, watering, fertilizing, replanting, deadheading, weeding, mulching, pest control, and acute frustration. This became especially apparent in the summer of 2011, when according to the National Climatic Data Center, climatologists declared that Oklahoma had suffered through the hottest summer ever recorded in the United States. Here in Oklahoma City, we experienced *57 days over 100°F* (38°C) in that calendar year. Add that to the record-breaking drought and you can see the gardeners' dilemma.

It is the primary reason I relegate most of my color, and work, to the cooler seasons of spring and fall. What seasonal color I *do* plant lasts longer, looks better, and gives me a much greater return on my investment of time and money whether in the potager or flower beds. It is a perfect example of executing one of the principles of Good Garden Fit that I discussed on page 51, gardening in the context of your geography and climate.

I also think that color selection and preferences depend on our personal relationship with color. A radiologist friend of mine embraces color in every way possible. In her decor, in her wardrobe and, of course, in her garden. Spending so many hours and years in her professional world with black and white imagery and reading x-rays and medical records compels her to gravitate to color in every aspect of her personal life. Conversely, I have read countless accounts of fashion and interior designers who work so much with color and pattern during the day that they crave neutral tones and calming hues in their homes and gardens as a visual respite when away from work.

My own relationship to color is highly influenced by my having grapheme-color synesthesia. Don't worry, it's not deadly nor contagious, though it is thought to be hereditary. There are multiple types of synesthesia, all with different symptoms. Grapheme-color synesthesia, what I have, is where you connect letters and days of the week with colors and is maybe the most common form. But there's also sound-to-color synesthesia, number-form, taste-color, and many others. A person may have only one type, or a combination of a few kinds. Studies show that perhaps 2–4 percent of the population are synesthetes, and it is prevalent in creative disciplines, such as music, design, and art.

For as long as I can remember, every number and every letter in the alphabet has been associated with a very specific color or hue of color, in some cases even gender. You can ask me today what color P is—by the way, it is the color of an orange calendula *(Calendula officinalis)*—and I would give you the exact same answer twenty years from now, or twenty years ago for that matter. I could even come up with a very unique color monograph for your name based on the letters used to spell it. I read recently that an artist is doing just that and creating and selling them as very personal gifts. I love the novelty behind this idea. I've often wondered if my preference for a more limited color palette in the garden is because I have so much verbal and written "color" constantly spinning in my head!

Of all the colors in the garden, green and all its iterations is my favorite garden color, and it is

A late summer bouquet for the cook. Romantic is the language of these zinnias *(Zinnia elegans)*, daisies *(Bellis perennis)*, phlox, globe amaranth *(Gomphrena globosa)*, and crape myrtle *(Lagerstroemia)* blooms and buds. The palette of these lovelies is feminine and delicate, but the plants themselves are tough, easy to grow, and perfect for southern gardens with intense heat and humidity.

a much undervalued one, I think. No color is more restful as a foil to others or brings more harmony, order, and sophisticated restraint to a garden. No matter how restrained, I find gardens with a preponderance of hues so dark as to read "black" neither fashionable, nor trendy—merely depressing despite its popularity in some gardening circles. Gray on the other hand is mysterious and increasingly intriguing to me. It communicates exotic climes and geography—the Mediterranean, Middle East, North Africa, and California. Figs and rosemary, olive trees and tarragon, artichokes, and curry—in the garden and in the kitchen . . . or a restaurant. In the brutal heat of a hot Oklahoman summer, plants in gray are soothing and provide a reason and rationale for enduring the hot temperatures—rewards such as spicy flavors, heady fragrance, and sensory succulence in both kitchen and garden.

COLOR TRENDS AND UNDERTONES

Every year, the color experts at Pantone announce a color pick for the year based on a selection from a group of more than twenty hues in their Fashion Trend Color palettes. Though gardeners in general aren't slavish about following trends, I do find certain colors come in and out of favor in garden circles.

In the latter part of the 1960s, orange was hot inside and out and had another resurgence in popularity at the end of the century. Yellow and purple seem to be having their moment now, and the popularity of all-white and all-green gardens persists. I find it interesting that the yellow and gold Pantone color selections for 2021 are both cheery and warm in temperament. Color may just be our sixth sense and an emotional expression of what we crave and need at that moment in time. If we need

I can't begin to calculate how many undertones are in this variety of camellia, but I know for sure that certain pinks wouldn't look good with it.

This household of gardeners infuses color into their gardenscapes with colorful porch furnishings, garden art, and huge doses of whimsy.

to be cheered up and warmly comforted, let those colors be one of our benefactors.

All yellows are not equal of course, nor pinks or reds or blues as we gardeners discover when we try to use simply "pink" or "purple" in the garden. I once tore out the contents of a beautiful "pink" window box I had just planted because the varying shades of "pink" kept fighting each other. And a window box is way too small for such arguments. As I have come to understand it, all colors have a mass tone, the color you directly see, and an undertone, which may not be readily apparent. Anyone who has picked out the wrong shade of a lipstick or foundation at the makeup counter knows exactly what I mean. Nothing ruins a good makeover, or garden design, more than clashing undertones.

Seeing undertones does not come naturally to me; I have to look for them. And the closer the clashing undertones are in proximity in the garden, the more dramatic the clash . . . as in my window box. In other areas of my garden, where space diffuses the tension, it is not a problem. Or at least it doesn't bother me as much. I have learned over time to take a petal or a leaf I am trying to arrange a marriage for to the nursery with me. Or gather candidates at the nursery together side by side to see if they are compatible with one another before making a purchase.

In the kitchen garden, color is a more nuanced consideration, generally consisting of lots of green with lots of pops of color—squash, tomatoes, eggplant, and peppers. More concerned are we with feeding our culinary appetites than our visual ones. But as in Rosemary Verey's potager, when great attention is taken to color harmony even in the vegetable garden, a true masterpiece can be created. For one particular magazine shoot, I took a petal from a rudbeckia (*Rudbeckia hirta*) to the paint store for them to re-create the hue as closely as possible. I then painted my garden bench in the same area to match the rudbeckia blooms and the effect was magical—with no disagreeable undertones. The same could be done with a small bench near the tomato patch or a stool near the bush beans.

Colored plant supports and stakes can easily be found in a variety of colors to add a punch of color to your potager, but when using them, I try to stick to just one or two colors. Confetti gardening with too much busyness detracts from the whole in my humble opinion. But again, if it gives you joy and *is* your style, by all means, follow your heart and ignore my red stop sign.

Mother Nature often lends a hand in providing just the artful pop of color we need right where we can most appreciate it.

The textures in this finial, along with the foamy green of the baby apples *(Malus domestica)* and the yellow-green of spring's emerging foliage, are as enticing and alluring as the brightest of color combinations.

THE PLAY OF LIGHT AND COLOR

Repeat after me: *It's all about the light. It's all about the light. It's all about the light.*

Because it is, and the longer you garden and the more theatrically and elegantly you want your garden to evolve, the more attention you must pay to the quality of light at different times of the day, of the season, and of the year.

I always request, whenever possible, that visitors come early or late in the day, seldom if ever in late summer, and never in the middle of a record-breaking hot and dry summer. Why? Because the quality of light is so poor and harsh and unflattering at certain times of day and times of the year that I don't want to do injustice to the usual beauty of the garden or the gardener who designed and maintains it—regardless of how well pruned and primped and garden tour ready it might be at the time. Photographers know that there is a golden hour for a reason—to take pictures when the light is the softest, the most alluring, and the most flattering. When the play of light is at its most glorious, on a golden day in fall, or a misty morning in the spring, our gardens can surpass even our most lofty ambitions for an elegant garden, edible or not.

While we can't control the intensity of sunlight in our respective longitudes and latitudes, we can control other things that affect the quality of light in our gardens. In my own garden, I think almost everything, sun-loving edibles and sweaty gardeners among them, would benefit from high dappled shade on hot and steamy summer afternoons. To a great degree, that is something I *can* control by judicious pruning and decreasing the density of a tree canopy. Not only does this improve and increase the quality of light, but it can make a claustrophobic space seem more open, less buggy, and more inviting overall.

One of the reasons I so love boxwood, hollies, and other glossy evergreens is because of the way they catch and reflect light. Their shiny leaves glisten when catching sunlight, so much so that their reflective qualities can even help illuminate a dark space. Contrasting a waxy, shiny leaf with a matte fuzzy one is not only an interesting textural move, but also another way to play with light. The one captures and reflects light, while the other captures and absorbs it—an appealing and intriguing pairing. The next time you visit a garden, try to deconstruct why some compositions grab your eye. Just try not to visit at high noon.

COMPOSITION

If color is about emotion, mood, personality, and light, composition is about texture, form, numbers, and placement. Along with color, we gardeners try to compose a symphony of plantings that is pleasing to the eye and soul. Composition, that interplay between light and dark, smooth, and rough, matte, and glossy, bold and demure, is often that synergistic element that we can't quite put our finger on, but that transforms something pretty into something memorable and amazing. A true garden orchestration.

Creating effective compositions is one of the most entertaining and enjoyable facets of gardening, I think. Nothing is more fun to me than going to my local nursery or garden center and putting together an arrangement of plants—edible and ornamental—that will have a wonderful conversation with one another and produce a fabulous display. If the aesthetics of a container—terracotta or concrete, glazed or matte—factors into the equation, it's all the more fun.

For example, today I went to a home improvement store in search of light bulbs and S hooks. I "accidentally" also came home with an assortment of plants I thought would make an interesting combination in a hanging basket—a LARGE hanging basket I might add—in my potager. As seems to be the trend for my personal garden this year, my muse was purple, specifically in the form of the deep purple of a 'Thai' basil (*Ocimum basilicum* var. *thyrsiflora*) bloom. That basil told me that it would like to be escorted to a garden event by a 'Sun Golden' coleus (*Coleus scutellarioides* 'Sun Golden') edged in purple. The event is a hanging basket festival showcasing a *Loropetalum* Red Diamond™, accompanied by a purple bell pepper (*Capsicum*

annuum) and a lime green Shishito chilli pepper (*Capsicum annuum*). I think a trailing, light lavender, annual bloomer should be added to spill out over the edge and it might be just the right additional flowery guest for scintillating conversation. I did decide to invite some purple basil I had already started from seed, and before I knew it, we had a party going. So many combos, so little time! Who am I to deny them their summer of bliss and a really good time?

HANDHELD, TUSSIE-MUSSIE DESIGN

According to Wikipedia, "the term *tussie-mussie* (also tussy-mussy) comes from the reign of Queen Victoria (1837–1901), when small handheld bouquets or nosegays became a popular fashion accessory. Typically, tussie-mussies include floral symbolism from the language of flowers, and therefore may be used to send a message to the recipient." My interest in them comes more from practical design considerations. If a combination of foliage and flowers looks pleasing and resonates in my hand-held bouquet (and can grow well and thrive together in my garden beds), then I have a good planting scheme in the works. The combination of foliage and flowers will also look comely in the vase, I might add.

Right: If a combination of foliage looks beautiful in a handheld bouquet, chances are it will resonate equally as well in the garden. Note how important the role of colorful foliage is in this fall ensemble.

Opposite: The matte large foliage of this *esculentus* 'Cowhorn' okra (*Abelmoschus esculentus* 'Cowhorn') looks great with the tiny-leaved glossy boxwood. During a very hot summer, it also provides a bit of shade with its umbrella form.

Tomato cages in a bright yellow add a bit of color to a mostly green tableau. Their color mimics the color of the golden plants in the area.

This union between 'Orange Rocket' barberry (*Berberis thunbergii* 'Orange Rocket') and 'Royal Sunset' lily (*Lilium* 'Royal Sunset') makes for a delicate and effective marriage of two burnt coral companions. A flashy golden barberry adds spice to the marriage.

I once painted a garden bench to be the exact same golden yellow hue as these sunflowers *(Helianthus)* and black-eyed Susans *(Rudbeckia hirta)*. The basket holding these blooms, a treasure of mine, was made by one of my sisters out of grape vine growing on her property.

THE IMPORTANCE OF COLOR ECHOES

One of my favorite expressions and applications in gardening is the phrase *color echoes*, when the color of one plant or parts of a plant repeats or echoes a similar color in a different plant or even a fixture or feature in the garden. Creating color echoes establishes a sense of harmony in your garden and brings out colors, features, and shades that weren't previously visible. Subtle or bold, color echoes can manifest themselves in shrubs, trees,

> "NATURE ALWAYS WEARS
> THE COLORS OF THE SPIRIT."
> —RALPH WALDO EMERSON, *NATURE*

perennials, annuals, stems, leaves, bark, petals, and garden ornaments and art. By looking closely into the soul of a hollyhock (*Alcea*) or the well of a calla lily (*Zantedeschia aethiopica*), you can identify a world of color that is repeated and mirrored elsewhere in the garden to magical effect and in imaginative, personal ways.

EAT THE RAINBOW

A restricted palette in color design is one thing, but a restricted color palette in our diets is entirely another—and potentially dangerous to our health and well-being. I find it ironic that junk food suppliers spend so much money on research and enticing color palettes in packaging to motivate customers to buy their products. As if all that fat and salt and sugar was not enticing and addictive enough. Mother Nature, with a lot of help from hybridizers over the years, has color in her packaging down to a science, so to speak. So much so that we are encouraged to be healthy by *eating the rainbow* of her offerings: red pepper (*Capsicum annuum*), orange carrots (*Daucus carota subsp. sativus*),

yellow squash (*Cucurbita pepo*), leafy greens, blueberries (*Vaccinium*), indigo eggplant (*Solanum melongena*), and violet turnips (*Brassica rapa subsp. rapa*)—all compliments of Dr. Roy G Biv and his sequence of hues making up the rainbow.

I admit falling prey to the former colorful promotions, but I am equally enticed by the latter. I am a sucker for anything natural and beautiful, and nothing is more beautiful to me than platters, tiered stands, and baskets filled to overflowing with fresh fruits and vegetables. The only thing more beautiful and enticing? When those fruits and vegetables have leaves, branches, and stems still attached to designate their freshness and evoke their beautiful natural growing habitat and geography—at least in my imagination.

Eating the Rainbow

RED
HEALTH BENEFITS:
ANTI-INFLAMMATORY, ANTIOXIDANT, MAY HELP LOWER RISK OF HEART DISEASE AND CERTAIN CANCERS, MAY HELP REDUCE SUN-RELATED SKIN DAMAGE

YELLOW AND ORANGE
HEALTH BENEFITS:
ANTI-INFLAMMATORY, ANTIOXIDANT, SUPPORTS EYE HEALTH, MAY HELP LOWER RISK OF HEART DISEASE AND CANCER

GREEN
HEALTH BENEFITS:
ANTI-INFLAMMATORY, ANTIOXIDANT, CRUCIFEROUS VEGGIES IN PARTICULAR MAY HELP LOWER RISK OF HEART DISEASE AND CERTAIN CANCERS

BLUE AND PURPLE
HEALTH BENEFITS:
ANTI-INFLAMMATORY, ANTIOXIDANT, MAY HELP IMPROVE BRAIN FUNCTION, MAY HELP LOWER RISK OF HEART DISEASE, NEUROLOGICAL DISORDERS, TYPE 2 DIABETES, AND CERTAIN CANCERS

DARK RED
HEALTH BENEFITS:
ANTI-INFLAMMATORY, ANTIOXIDANT, MAY HELP SUPPORT ATHLETIC PER-FORMANCE THROUGH INCREASED OXYGEN UPTAKE, MAY HELP LOWER RISK OF HIGH BLOOD PRESSURE, HEART DISEASE, AND CERTAIN CANCERS

WHITE AND BROWN
HEALTH BENEFITS:
ANTI-INFLAMMATORY, ANTIOXIDANT, MAY HELP LOWER RISK OF HEART DISEASE, COLON CANCER, AND OTHER CANCERS
SOURCE: HEALTHLINE.COM/NUTRITION/ EAT-THE-RAINBOW

Leafy greens, radishes, sorrel, and chard—just some of the rainbow options at Guilford Gardens, a local CSA and urban farm. Rich, gorgeous colors to satisfy both visual and gastronomic appetites.

Beauty alone won't entice us to consume more fruits and vegetables of different colors on a daily basis, however. Deliciousness is paramount, whether you are a finicky five-year old or a thirty-year-old soccer mom. All the more reason to eat our produce when it is at peak of season and its most succulent—not shipped in from halfway around the world midwinter.

And let's be realistic, eating the rainbow, unlike opening a bag of chips or pouring sugary cereal into a bowl, can require more time and preparation. Even if it is as simple as washing greens for dinner, peeling carrots, or cutting through the hard rind of a squash. Convenience, so prioritized in our busy lives, has made us lazy as well as less healthy. I speak from personal experience. Good habit formation in eating healthily cannot be overstated.

For example, I know if I don't wash my greens from the garden or my grocer early in the day, I will be too unmotivated to do so right before dinner. The same holds true for roasting my red peppers, prepping my green beans, dicing my onions, and washing my brussels sprouts. For you, the exact opposite may be true. In either case, produce preparation and planning is equally as important as garden prep and planning. After all, the whole point is to grow what we eat and eat what we grow, not grow what we *think* we will consume and then throw it in the compost pile, uneaten and unappreciated.

A true gardening lifestyle experience helps me not only eat healthier, consuming vital phyto-nutrients, fiber, vitamins, and minerals, but also encourages good habit formation and discipline. The garden gives in many ways if we are receptive to its lessons.

EXPLOSION OF COLOR SALAD

I remember the first time I had a salad like this as if it were yesterday. I was single and in my twenties, going to a picnic at the home of another single gal in her twenties. When she brought a *huge bowl* of the most beautiful, colorful, fresh salad I had ever seen to the table, well, let's just say I was beyond impressed. And slightly (okay very) jealous that she had the panache and the homegrown garden goods to produce such a masterpiece at such a tender age—did I mention we were both single and in our twenties? It wasn't only the presentation of such a culinary marvel, it was the effort, the thought, and the graciousness behind it. Vibrant edible flowers—violas, pansies (*Viola* x *wittrockiana*), calendula (*Calendula officinalis*), chive blossoms (*Allium schoenoprasum*)—were scattered gaily (yes *gaily*, I could tell) over a bed of fresh greens. The greens were arugula (*Eruca vesicaria ssp. sativa*), tiny chard (*Beta vulgaris* ssp. *cicla*) leaves, butter lettuce (*Lactuca sativa var. capitata*), or maybe a mesclun mix. And then a beautiful vinaigrette was served on the side. And did I mention it was served on a cobalt blue platter? I don't remember if it was or was not served with a perfectly chilled rosé with a warm sourdough loaf and heaps of butter or not, but I digress.

It was memorable, sensational, and now that I am older, wiser, and a gardener myself, I know that it was not that difficult to compose and create. The next time you want to impress the socks off someone of *any* age, just serve a salad of colorful garden jewels.

Toss and serve a nice vinaigrette over fresh greens of your choice. Sliced scallions optional. Garnish with edible flowers and serve additional dressing on the side. (Note: Use only flowers that have not been sprayed with pesticides or other chemicals. Use as few or as many as you like.)

It's been my experience that the treat is more visual than tasty, but there *is* flavor to each variety to a greater or lesser degree. I have heard it said that greens taste like they smell, and that's a good description. Experiment, but only consume what you know is 100 percent safe to eat. If you want maximum pleasure from this floriferous salad, serve it to a child and see their eyes and curiosity light up.

Edible Blooms

Many varieties of flowers are edible, including:
- Violas, pansies
- Chive blossoms
- Nasturtiums
- Lavender
- Squash blooms
- Daylily buds (*Hemerocallis fulva*)
- Hibiscus
- Calendula a.k.a. pot marigold
- Violets
- Jasmine

Try using them in teas, cocktails, and salads. Serve as a garnish on cakes or cheeses. Use in baked desserts or frozen into ice cubes or ice cream. Blend into creamy cheeses, spreads, and tapenades.

Top left to right: dahlia, spilanthes, gladiolus, sunflower, butterfly pea, tuberous begonia, bachelor buttons, nasturtium, garden phlox

The flavor of each of these edible blooms is as distinctive as their color, shape, and size. Such a fun way to challenge and excite your taste buds!

PART III
MOTIVATION

"THERE IS IN FACT NO DISTINCTION BETWEEN THE FATE OF
THE LAND AND THE FATE OF THE PEOPLE.
WHEN ONE IS ABUSED, THE OTHER SUFFERS."
—WENDELL BERRY

"HERE IS A PLACE WE DID NOT HARVEST OR PLUNDER BUT
ALLOWED IT TO ENRICH AND TO INSPIRE US OVER MANY GENERATIONS.
NOT ONLY DID WE CARE ABOUT THIS PLACE, WE CARED FOR IT.
WE DEFENDED IT AND STILL DO . . . THIS IS STEWARDSHIP."

—KIM HEACOX

Chapter 7

GARDEN STEWARDSHIP

GARDEN RESPONSIBLY

What exactly does it mean to be a good steward of the land, more specifically, *your* land and *your* garden and edible landscape? To use an admonition from campers and scout leaders, it means to leave the campsite or land better than you found it, and as the medical community might say, *first do no harm.* To that I would add that good gardeners are not only responsible stewards of the land and soil itself but are also responsible consumers of the resources used to manage our gardens and landscapes. Living and gardening in an area that experiences frequent periods of drought, incredible heat, and extreme weather has made me especially mindful of this. As climate change escalates and water consumption goes up with increasing demand, desertification or lower productivity of the land is becoming more and more common and begins to threaten previously unimaginable areas. This trend impacts our gardens and how we tend them that much more greatly, not to mention how well we gardeners sleep at night. It's sad but probably true that most of us finally have our epiphany and aha! revelation about our environment, our planet, and all creatures that inhabit it when it *becomes personal and problematic for and to us.*

Take ownership of caring for the garden you tend by learning, watching, listening, and engaging.

It becomes personal to all of us when our water bill skyrockets along with our electric bill in the summer. It becomes personal when our gardens don't produce or perform the way they used to. It becomes personal when we realize the fireflies that enchanted us as children are now infrequent and special in some areas. It becomes personal when nonnative plants planted by a previous owner of our home now threaten to take over our backyards . . . and front yards . . . and strangle us in our beds at night. When it is personal to us or a bird species we love is threatened with extinction, then we typically begin to care, take action, and become better stewards of our gardens and our earth. I am as guilty as anyone of this environmental malfeasance. But I am trying to mend my ways. When I started gardening over thirty years ago, I gave little thought to gardening organically, planting natives, saving water, or not jeopardizing pollinators when I was spraying for bud worms. Now, a day rarely goes by without my wondering if this or that practice is eco-logically wise, organically sound, and quite frankly, more effective than less earth-friendly alternatives.

TAKE OWNERSHIP

In his thought-provoking book *Nature's Best Hope: A New Approach to Conservation That Starts in Your Yard*, Douglas W. Tallamy reiterates this thought and promotes the common-sense "let's all take ownership of our planet" vision of a grassroots-level approach to conservation and good environmental practices. He literally brings home the idea of private individual accountability and responsibility for conservation and wildlife habitat preservation. He maintains that actionable concern shouldn't just happen *over there* in national and state parks, wildlife preserves, and animal refuges and then implemented by the government, environmental groups, and nature advocacy organizations. On the contrary, his approach concentrates the power and initiative right in the hands of us gardeners, homeowners, and *anyone* interested in bringing home good environmental practices. After all, it seems only right and obvious that good environ-mental stewardship and concern for our planet should start at home with us as individuals, families, communities, and mentors.

Being a responsible garden steward means more than just using organic fertilizers and throwing your banana peel into the holly hedge. Listed below are some of the things we can do to be responsible gardeners. If the list seems daunting, just start *somewhere* with *something* and then build on it. Better practices can become better habits—a gardening mantra I repeat daily—and sometimes even put into practice. Don't let the perfect be the enemy of the good. And if you are an organic gardening absolutist, don't shame those who are not but who are trying to be more cognizant of their role in a healthy planet.

Drip irrigation waters plants right at the root zone. Strategic placement of the drip line is important as is line maintenance to ensure the line remains clog free and in good working condition.

Major change begins on the margins of our behaviors. When we know better and learn more, we do better. Our role as garden teachers has never been more important in the causation of behavioral change.

PRACTICE GOOD GARDEN STEWARDSHIP: WHAT EACH OF US CAN DO

1. Be water wise.

Manage and monitor your water consumption. Pay attention to community guidelines for water usage. Water in the cool of the morning when transpiration and evaporation are less and water pressure is normally the highest. Wherever possible, water at the root zone and avoid wasteful water runoff from irrigation systems. Look for alternatives to water hogs, such as huge expanses of lawn and plant selections inappropriate to your zone. Water according to weather conditions. In-ground irrigation systems that water based on automatic time settings with no regard to actual weather events can be not only wasteful and irresponsible but can even cause more harm than good. Infrequent, deep watering is encouraged instead of frequent, shallow watering, which encourages shallow-rooted lawns, shrubs, and ornamentals, as well as edibles, to grow. And always follow the commandment to *know thy climate, geography, local weather, and growing zone.* High wind, intense heat, longer days under searing sun, and native soils with poor moisture retention all affect watering schedules. Being a daughter of the Great Plains of the United

States, home to the Dust Bowl of the first half of the twentieth century, I am also very aware of the ways heat and wind wick away precious moisture from unplanted, unprotected barren soil. Not only is invaluable moisture lost, but also life-sustaining topsoil and crucial erosion control elements.

I myself plead guilty to being an inveterate over-waterer. At the first signs of wilting and heat stress, I grab for my hose like a cowboy with a fast draw. Neither is a good idea, and both can be deadly. Learn to be attentive and know the difference between a plant that is truly thirsty and one that is just hot and unhappy.

Most plants will go limp when temperatures are high and the sun at its brightest. After a particularly cloudy and rainy spring this year, nearly every plant in my garden looked droopy and deflated when the sun finally decided to arrive, even without the heat. When the sun *and* heat made their seasonal presence known, the entire garden began to gasp at the intensity of it all but not *always* for water. Like our own blinking eyes as we emerge from a dark cave and adapt to the light, so must our plants adjust to extreme changes that happen suddenly without the opportunity to slowly acclimate.

While watering more is a summer gardening ritual for most of us, especially for container plantings, it is not always lack of moisture that causes distress. As I write this, I can look out the French doors of my office to a bed of hydrangeas across the lawn. They look as bereft and saggy as can be in today's high heat. But I know we had rain earlier in the week, sufficient rain to meet their needs. Consequently, I will leave them be, along with my hose and a gardener's inclination to run to their

Top: These good-looking water barrels are on my wish list as soon as I can find a place for them.

Bottom: This drip line watering system that irrigates the plant directly at the root zone is both efficient and time saving. Still, calibrating the rate of the drip and the least amount of water the plant needs to thrive requires lots of observation, modifications as weather conditions change, and line maintenance.

rescue. By this evening when temps cool a bit and shade arrives, they will perk up again, along with countless other plants in my garden suffering heat stroke right along with them.

So how much and how often *should* you water, you ask? That I cannot say, as my growing situation may differ greatly from yours. It also depends on what type of gardening you do, what ornamentals and edibles you grow, and the condition and moisture retention of your soil. Nothing can take the place of observation, researching watering topics for your zone, and knowing the needs of the plants you grow. However, as a general rule, always plan to water more as plants are getting established, when temperatures soar, when winds are high, and if you rely heavily on container gardening.

2. Avoid harmful chemicals and embrace imperfection.

Most of us are now familiar with the harmful effects of pesticides and herbicides on human health and the health and sustainability of wildlife, pollinators, beneficial insects, and the soil itself. Excessive, irresponsible use of insecticides and fungicides, especially to maintain a perfect lawn, may seem obvious, but excessive use of fertilizers may not be as intuitive. Heavy rains and too much watering can cause excess pest control chemicals, fungicides, and fertilizer run off into sewer systems and all manner of bodies of water. This not only affects water quality but can also cause uncontrolled growth of algae and aquatic vegetation from high levels of nitrogen (N) and phosphorus (P). When algae die and sink to the bottom of a pond or lake, this often leads to oxygen depletion resulting in the harm or destruction of aquatic life.

Conversely, during periods of intense drought, chemicals, salts, and toxins can build up in the soil. Without rain or adequate water to dilute the amendments, soak them in, and leech them out of the soil, concentrations can build up to dangerously high levels. In addition, with little or no rainfall and water-soluble nutrients in the soil, nutrients remain unavailable to your plants and may wash away during the next rainfall, especially in areas with sparse vegetation—like that barren area under your tree where grass won't grow.

I can sympathize with demanding, fastidious gardeners who strive for perfection, unblemished fruits and vegetables, and fungal-free lawns. I count myself among you. But I am learning to embrace imperfection. Sure, sometimes insecticidal soap won't be as effective or as deadly as something far more toxic, but if I am going to *eat* that hole-y head of greens or less-than-perfect peach, I am good with that. Very good with that. Same goes for my somewhat chewed bouquet of sunflowers and zinnias, though I just plan on cutting rather than consuming them. I am even sparing with my organic dusts and sprays. Insecticidal soaps, neem oil, *Bacillus thuringiensis*, and spinosad can't always discriminate between the good guys and the bad guys, and to save the good, I will often give the bad more leeway.

By employing organic garden techniques and integrated pest management, we can help to insure the health of our gardens, our communities, and our own health and well being.

Use technology to identify and combat pests! Use phone apps to identify plant and pest diseases. These apps can turn your phone into a mobile crop doctor to accurately detect pests and diseases on crops within seconds. Apps are also available to help identify the plants and flowers themselves. These apps come in multiple languages and are easy to use from the convenience of your hand-held device.

Jumping spiders like this one do not spin webs but rather stalk and pounce on their prey. To attract them into your garden space, mulch your plants to provide spiders with more humidity and an enticing habitat.

Most people recognize ladybugs as a beneficial bug that can help control aphids. They also can help eliminate mites, scale, thrips, and whiteflies.

Robber flies and their larvae help control beetles, leafhoppers, and grasshoppers. Attract robber flies to your garden by planting flowers that bloom throughout the growing season, such as zinnias.

The cocoon of an ichneumon wasp delicately hanging from a leaf. Parasitic wasps help control garden pests such as cutworms, tomato hornworms, and other caterpillars.

Hoverflies are bee mimics that can serve as pollinators, but, more importantly, their larvae can control up to 70–100 percent of aphid infestations. To attract them to your garden, plant oregano, garlic chives, and alyssum.

Integrated Pest Management

Integrated pest management (IPM) is a sustainable, science-based, decision-making process that combines biological, cultural, physical, and chemical tools to identify, manage, and reduce risk from pests and pest management tools and strategies in a way that minimizes overall economic, health, and environmental risks. You can learn more about IPM by visiting the IPM Institute of America's website: ipminstitute.org.

Praying mantis are a great benefit to the garden by helping to control aphids, mosquitos, caterpillars, beetles, grasshoppers, and crickets.

Make It Personal

Keri, the Bug Whisperer, shares her own IPM experiences in her small urban garden

I believe in having a balance in the garden and letting nature play its course as much as possible. When planning my garden, I incorporated marigolds, borage, and nasturtium to attract pollinators and beneficial insects. A few weeks into planting my spring garden, my lettuce bolted, and the delicate yellow flowers were so pretty I could not bring myself to pull it up. Not long after, hoverflies started to appear in my garden.

In the past couple of months, I have seen earthworms, spiders, praying mantis, picture wing flies, cabbage moths and their caterpillars, and whiteflies. None of these populations have gotten out of control. Once the borage grew larger, I noticed I no longer had cabbage worms on my kale. (I have also been told it can repel the dreaded tomato hornworm.) I sprayed the whiteflies with streams of water a few times and they have since disappeared. In the past, I have taken measures to control pests on my plants and have found no better cure than being patient and watching the cycle of insects

My friend Keri delights in the beauty and fascination of bugs the way I do in seedheads and blooms.

remedy issues. For example, leaving aphids so that ladybug and hoverfly larvae have plenty to eat!

Using sprays and even organic methods of insect control may disrupt a food source for beneficials or unintentionally wipe them out. From time to time, I will relocate a nuisance pest if it is getting too aggressive (e.g., slugs or snails to the compost pile or tapping the underside of a leaf to bounce a grasshopper out of the garden). Time will tell if this method continues to work for me as the summer wears on, but for now I am pleased with the balance of nature I have in my garden. I even have my own resident garden spider that is very happy to patrol from the top of my lavender.

Regardless of the scale of your composting efforts, every little bit helps keep organic waste out of the landfill and transform it into black gold. All for free!

4. Improve garden drainage.

Well-draining soil is the holy grail to any of us who garden in heavy clay and compacted soil. Rainfall that percolates down into the subsoil naturally waters our gardens and replenishes groundwater. Good drainage prevents root rot, encourages healthy root penetration, and prevents pockets of standing water that encourage mosquitoes and other pests. Adding organic matter to both heavy clay soil or sandy, gritty soil helps the earth retain moisture and encourages healthy root growth and happy plants.

5. Plant a variety of flowers, herbs, and edibles.

Provide a banquet for pollinators and beneficial insect life. Take advantage of flowers and herbs that work double and triple duty throughout the garden by deterring pests, feeding the soil, and encouraging good bugs. Jessica Walliser's book *Plant Partners: Science-Based Companion Planting Strategies for the Vegetable Garden* is a comprehensive resource for planning and planting synergistic combinations to reduce disease, reduce pests, improve soil fertility, and support pollinators. Books and resources such as this are a wonderful form of continuing education for gardeners.

3. Composting turns trash into treasure.

Composting, on any scale, is one of the best ways to keep valuable organic material out of landfills and create nutrient-rich amendment, black gold, at the same time. Even small gardens like mine can accommodate a compost tumbler on the driveway or a small composting system in an unused space on your property. A friend of mine keeps a covered scrap bowl for compostable kitchen waste by her back door with a small garden trowel. Periodically, she just buries the waste wherever she finds a spot receptive to her digging! In situ composting it is.

Some ingenious gardeners even find ways to make the compost heap attractive and stylish—another place for planting when cultivation space is at a premium for growing edibles, herbs, and flowers.

6. Plant trees and encourage areas for wildlife habitat.

Planting deciduous and evergreen trees invites wildlife and pollinators by providing shelter, food, and habitat. Fallen leaves provide material for mulching and composting, and fruiting, flowering, and medicinal plants prove invaluable everywhere in the home. Trees that are artfully and carefully pruned contribute not only shade and ambiance to the garden but also contribute to the design, mood, and sensibility of the garden. On a practical level, shade trees can reduce energy costs, physically protect you from the damaging effects of the sun, and increase the market value of your home and the neighborhood, as a whole.

Plant a variety of plants to attract beneficials and wildlife to your garden. Extra credit if you color coordinate.

This garden is a natural haven for brilliant red cardinals in the winter . . . a true four-season garden for people and wildlife alike.

7. Share the wealth.

Being a good garden steward includes contributing to the health of the community as well as the land you cultivate and the very planet itself. Sharing the abundance you create through your garden labor—be it produce, flowers, seeds, cuttings, volunteering, and even sharing the knowledge you acquire—is a wonderful way to contribute to the welfare of your neighborhood, city, and even larger communities. You may have a small garden, but it can play a big role in the health and vitality of the environment and community in which you live. Most importantly, you are playing a vital part in the health and vitality of the planet itself, the only one we have, at least for now.

To create a garden that spans all four seasons is to create a whole new world for yourself and others. It's a way to live a life of joy, responsibility, accountability, and great riches.

Recommended Plants to Attract Butterflies and Other Pollinators

Lantana (top left): a must-have in the butterfly garden. Thrives in full sun and blooms prolifically all season.

Gaillardia (top middle): the state flower in Oklahoma and native to prairies across the United States. These colorful perennials require minimal care.

Coreopsis (top right): an easy-to-grow perennial with vibrant blooms that last from early spring until frost.

Asclepias (bottom left): the host plant for many caterpillars including the magnificent monarch. It's best to plant species native to your area if possible.

Zinnia (bottom middle): a pollinator magnet!

Cosmos (bottom right): easy to grow from seed, are heat and drought tolerant, and have large stores of nectar that pollinators love.

Chapter 8

LIFESTYLE AND WELLNESS

GROW YOUR OWN

As I write this, I am on an icepack and nursing a bad back. Yes, I threw my back out—not from moving a too-heavy pot or improper body form while weeding out nutsedge or planting my okra. The blame for this most recent episode (it is a recurring problem) I put squarely at the feet, or at the keyboard as it were, of my computer. This gardening physique of mine is not accustomed to sitting in front of a screen for hours, with or without periodic stretching and coffee breaks. It is *accustomed* to working in the garden. Gardening is not just my hobby; it is the linchpin to my entire life.

One of the wonderful things about being a gardener is that exercise and movement are inherent to the activity. Bend! Lift! Push! Pull! Carry! Move! Dig! But moving from a sedentary position behind a desk for hours on end to heading outdoors to capture (from an incredibly awkward angle) a photograph of a chamomile blossom, well, that's when things get ugly, and you find yourself cuddling up to your ice pack and heating pad.

A couple of hours of gardening, much less a whole weekend, makes it easy to get in 10,000 steps a day, do plenty of resistance training, and burn up lots of calories to keep one's weight in check. No gym or weights required. Sitting in front of a computer screen, not so much. Gardening to me is a lifestyle choice that keeps me healthy mentally and physically. The garden is typically the focus of my day in one way or another—it is the nucleus to the atom of my life overall. When my life gets out of balance, and I don't have the time or conditions to garden,

My friend, fellow gardener, and chef Kamala Gamble off to feed her chickens.

Turning your overflowing-to-excess compost pile not only oxygenates all that organic matter but also provides great resistance exercise for the gardener, helping to build muscle and work off frustrations.

Victory Gardens

According to Wikipedia, victory gardens, also called war gardens or food gardens for defense, were "vegetable, fruit, and herb gardens planted at private residences and public parks in the US, United Kingdom, Canada, Australia, and Germany during WWI and WWII. In wartime, governments encouraged people to plant victory gardens to supplement their rations and boost morale. Besides indirectly aiding the war effort, these gardens were also considered a civil 'morale booster' in that gardeners could feel empowered by their contribution of labor and rewarded by the produce gown. This made victory gardens a part of daily life on the home front."

Living a garden life often means not worrying about your manicure when a garden chore has your name on it!

everything seems to get thrown off. Or out. Like my back. Or my mood. Or my healthy eating resolutions. That negative cascading effect doesn't just impact me and my own sense of equilibrium, it also affects those around me. My negativity is contagious and will infect my family and friends and anyone I encounter if I'm not careful. For these reasons, and countless others of course, I make gardening a priority in my life.

Truly, I live a garden-based life with the garden being at the very heart of it. You might be the same. I look at almost everything through a gardening lens. It is a wonderful metaphor for how to live a life, raise a family, treat your friends, and practice the golden rule. It also informs how I decorate my home, dress myself, engage with others, practice lifelong learning, select travel destinations, and give back to my community. Most importantly, it helps me allay my anxieties and put life's challenges in perspective.

And I am not the only one. Interest in gardening, and edible gardening in particular, has surged over the past couple of years during the COVID-19

Fresh lettuces, onions, and just-plucked beets from rain-dampened earth, whether from your own garden or a local farm or CSA, are part of a holistic gardening lifestyle.

pandemic. Anxiety over food security, job security, mental health, and even boredom drove many of us, first-time gardeners among us, to our gardens and gardening as a productive hobby. According to Google Trends, in March of 2020, interest in growing or starting a garden hit an all-time high. "Growing vegetables from scraps" as a search term was up 4,650 percent from the years past, and the hashtag #victorygardens found a whole new life on Instagram. My own social media platforms experienced huge growth as interest in gardening as a hobby sky-rocketed and new and experienced gardeners alike found more time and opportunities to pursue it.

Gardening, along with baking, organizing, and home improvement, became a way for us to relieve stress and anxiety and give us a sense of control over an uncontrollable situation. It's been proven that just being in a leafy green and outdoor space enhances our mood and slows the pace of our breathing. Businesses related to gardening, from

Guilford Gardens is a small urban farm in Oklahoma City run as a local family business. They cater meals and events, provide fresh organic produce to their customers, and grow their garden in the very heart of their family life. The quintessential gardening lifestyle!

seed sources to landscapers, no doubt experienced the same kind of euphoria and mood elevation as orders far exceeded expectations and business boomed.

Clearly, in an atmosphere of stress and worry, concern over food supply, and lots of time to fill, gardening seems a positive, no-brainer response. It is fun, educational, practical, kid friendly and relatively inexpensive in comparison to other hobbies. It helps us channel our inner kindergartener every time we see a seed germinate or a sow bug become a perfect roly-poly. Gardening gives us permission to be kids again. Not a bad thing under any circumstances.

More importantly, when we need the kind of comfort and support only nature can provide, gardening is literally out our back door. Or on the terrace. Or near a bright window. Gardening's accessibility makes it attractive and compelling. Research tells us that people with daily exposure to plants feel better, live longer, and even behave better than those who don't. There is hardly a social experience or business encounter, much less one more strip mall or massive parking lot, that isn't improved by more plants and more gardens.

YES, GARDENING IS A SPORT

In 2016, the Council of Europe defined "sport" to include all forms of physical exercise, including those done just for fun. Gardening, that means you! Gardening can be as rigorous or as relaxed as one chooses, but exercise it is. And like all athletic activity, gardening requires thoughtful warm-ups and cooldowns like any other sport to avoid injury and accident. Avid skiers prepare for ski season weeks in advance. Avid gardeners should do no less. It's a real tragedy to lose a whole gardening season to a torn disk, wrenched knee, or traumatized shoulder when some preventive measures could have been taken to avoid injury. I learned this the hard way after tearing a disk in 2001. Now that I know better, I do better! And physical preparation is now part of my seasonal and daily gardening routine.

Additional Helpful Tips to Remember

- Slowly work into gardening. Take breaks. It is a workout. Your body must adapt to it.
- Tighten abs when lifting, which helps with stability, strength, and power.
- Try to keep your body upright, back straight, and prevent hunching over to protect yourself from injury.
- Proper hamstring, back, and abdominal activation will prevent back injuries.
- Stay hydrated and drink plenty of water during the heat of the summer.

How to correctly lift a planter: Squat with tightened glutes and quads to pick something up, rather than just bending. Bring the object as close as possible to your chest with your elbows tucked in.

Gardening puts us in the flow, encourages mindfulness, and helps us commune and interact with nature and her rhythms.

Though it may not be an Olympic or college tuition-earning sport, *lots* of friendly rivalry and a competitive spirit exists in the gardening arena. But also, gardening has a spirit of community, commiseration, and comradery. Indeed, gardening *is* a sport—sharing all these things while also enhancing connections between friends, neighbors, families, generations, and disparate others who share the same values and interests. Values that relate to community, service, the beauty of our surroundings, and the health of our bodies and the environment. I think it is one of the most important elements in the pursuit of the collective good and our community's quality of life. I guess in many ways gardening is a team sport.

SHARING THE GARDEN

Any of us who takes great pains to make our gardens beautiful must admit to a certain degree of garden vanity. I know I do. Each year I plant almost 1,000 tulip bulbs in my front beds, along with masses of pansies, violas, phlox, chamomile, and cabbages. I do this mostly for myself because I love them so, but also for the benefit and enjoyment of the countless numbers who drive by my home each year and comment on the magnificence of the spring show. I bask in their compliments (as does my non-gardening husband, who savors the reflected glory while sitting on the front porch bench) and I am grateful for the privilege of sharing its beauty. But that's not the only reason. If I had a nickel for every time a car stopped to tell me that they drive by my home regularly—on their way to chemo, or to the doctor, or to pick up their kids from school—because it is a way to treat themselves in the process of doing something unpleasant, I would be a rich woman. These comments not only stroke my gardening vanity, but also feed my soul.

There were times when I thought my obsession with gardening might be a frivolous and superficial indulgence. Now I know better and am ever so aware of how much difference a garden can make in the lives of so many.

My old 1930s neighborhood is a congenial, walkable one. I have made countless friends and acquaintances because of the garden, as they walk by, ask questions, and visit a bit. One neighbor would drive by regularly. On one occasion, he told me that he had just been to Whole Foods Market, and now he was driving by my house. Both, he told me, were his happy places in the midst of his wife's cancer treatment. This past March a neighbor told me she was watching me crouch down, looking at the garden, in search of tulip tips and germinated seedlings. She called me the first sign of spring. Not a bad epitaph for a gardener, I think. To be called the first sign of spring in a happy place. I have been called worse.

Of course, what the garden does for us as a society and as a group, it does for us as individuals. My gateway drug to a full-blown gardening high and its therapeutically giddy effects was the standard '70s houseplant. In high school, a tumultuous and anxious time for nearly all of us, I would babysit in homes filled with spider plants, schefflera, and Swedish ivy. I found it wondrous and thrilling that I could start my own indoor garden with a single leaf from an African violet or a jade plant. I solicited some of those dangling spiders and leaves to add to my growing windowsill garden—a garden of great comfort and importance to me. The summer before I was to graduate high school, my family moved cross country to another state, another city, another school. Without friends or familiar faces, I turned to small trees and lush ferns growing in the woods behind our new home. They proved great company and wonderful companions. This became one of the first among many experiences where a form of gardening came to my rescue to help me through a difficult time.

A renewed interest in houseplants by young adults is now a familiar and nostalgic flashback. Millennials call it Plant Parenthood and are showing

Above: My daughter-in-law and my son give names to their plant children. Obviously, on this particular day, the kids were acting up! They have Vera Wang the Aloe, Misty the Monstera, Dan the Man, and Spike Lee the Snake Plant.

Opposite: I consider my spring garden a gift—to myself and any passersby who might appreciate it as a labor of love and a gift of the heart.

great enthusiasm for air plants, succulents, and other houseplants easily recognizable to anyone who ever visited a fern bar in their youth. My son and daughter-in-law have gone so far as to *name* their plant children, delighting in the selection of just the right moniker and how it reflects the personality of the plant. I too delight in their creativity, youthful enthusiasm, and their discovering the aesthetics of plants as part of one's decor and daily rounds.

Is it because young adults have put off having children, or rent rather than own, so they can't easily grow an outdoor garden? Or is it a much-needed reprieve from being hyper connected to technology, cyber living, and their devices? Does it matter? Not a bit. The trend is a positive one and they, like my generation before them, find gardening soothing, engaging, and relaxing. It's a small hop from this point to all-out gardening, growing herbs and veggies and flowers to become part of their daily rituals and a garden lifestyle of their own.

Garden Stories of Emotional Chlorophyll and Comfort

"My garden has always been a sanctuary for me. A place of wonder and discovery as well as my therapist in so many ways. Twelve years ago, it became my saving grace after experiencing a great loss in my life. My mother died the evening of the summer solstice and her death hit me like a freight train after her three-year battle with ovarian cancer. Nothing prepares you for such a loss. I spent that summer grieving her loss with every turn of the soil. I found myself talking to her, cursing at her for leaving me, and weeping every time a purple flower would come to life, her favorite color. There seemed to be an abundance of purple zinnias that year."

—Cheri Ruskus

"I process information while gardening—while working as a teacher, I remember so many spring and fall seasons when the days were long enough to work in the garden after work or on weekends, thinking about students and classroom dynamics while I worked. One young man was very bright and very deaf, with strong sign language skills, minimal English competence, and lots of frustration and anger. As I gardened, I tried to strategize how to help him. I wonder where he is now. Whether I was a constructive influence for him I don't know, but I remember thinking of his challenges while digging paths up the hill behind the azaleas."

—Dr. Terri Barrett

"One of my earliest childhood memories is picking flowers for my mom. She allowed me to pick flowering weeds in our yard for her; at that age, I did not know the difference. I just knew that she took the precious flowers from my tiny hands and selected a special vase in which to display them proudly. She loved her flowers.

"After buying a house of my own, I planted a variety of flowers my mom shared with me. I planted some of her favorites below the window of my guest bedroom, the room she later stayed in when she came to visit from assisted living. She would sit in a chair outside while I weeded her 'girls.'

"While she was in hospice care, I would bring her flowers from my garden, flowers once hers as well. On my way to the funeral home after her death, I gathered a small bouquet, wrapped in a wet paper towel. I walked in and the director, who knew and loved my mom, saw my little handheld bouquet. I said, 'I don't know what to do with these, but I needed to pick her one final bouquet.' She said, 'Give them to me . . .' When my sister and I walked nervously up to the casket, I saw that the funeral director had tucked them into Mom's hands. The last, but best bouquet I ever gave her."

—Dr. Meg Moorman

"I began my gardening journey about eight years ago, when my husband and I purchased a home with eight flower beds. It was enchanting to have blooms all around. Things flowered, like clockwork, one plant after the next as if they were on an intricately planned schedule. I knew very little about all the different species. I was thankful to have the internet, where I spent hours upon hours researching and discovering how to care for each plant. Working in the yard taught me how to slow down and appreciate the tiniest wonders and beauty of nature. I was inspired to go back to school and get a degree in horticulture. I have since quit my previous career that was unfulfilling and stressful. I am now fully immersed in the plant world, and I feel that I am flourishing as a person so much more than I ever have before."

—Keri Wilson

"Gardening is about lessons to me. You reap what you sow. Good soil makes for much fruit. Hard work yields a greater harvest. Compromise can be key. Space and time are limited. And blooms and fruit, like the connections they forge, are ephemeral. Savor them all."

—Dr. Barb Schroeder

PLANTING PROMISES AND
ANSWERED PRAYERS.
HEALING AND HOPE IN LONELINESS.
DYING BACK IN WINTER,
RESURRECTION IN SPRING.
A PLACE TO PONDER CREATION'S
MYSTERIES.
GOD REFLECTED
IN TINY BOUQUETS OF GLORY.
MY GARDEN.
—KAYE BATTLES

An especially powerful story about how gardening impacts one's life comes from my friend Nev. He struggles with epilepsy and has Asperger's syndrome. Both very different issues, but equally challenging. He shares that when he began gardening something amazing happened . . . as though he was transported to another realm and space. Slowly his health conditions started improving, a by-product he thinks of the tactile and sensory benefits of engaging and interacting with the garden. Amazingly, and I have seen this first-hand, he has not had an epileptic seizure in over a year and his sensory sensitivity issues are gone.

"The point is," he says, "gardening provides a no-cost prescription to healing. It opens your mind, warms your heart, and ignites your soul. All the medication and professional therapy in the world couldn't help me with the challenges I face due to epilepsy and Asperger's syndrome. But since planting my garden, I just feel so much better, and life is so much richer."

My young friend Julia is a whirling dervish of energy. But quiet moments of gardening with her grandmother help her to calm down, experience the miracles of seed germination, and practice mindful concentration.

PRIORITIZING GARDENING: PRACTICAL MATTERS

Prioritizing something is always a noble start. Now how do you execute and live out a priority with so many demands on your time, energy, and budget? Part of the Good Garden Fit concept I discussed on page 51 is figuring out how gardening fits into your daily habits, obligations, household expenses, and the framework of your life *as it exists now*. Like everything else in life, change is the only constant, and the number of resources you have to dedicate to living a gardening lifestyle will expand and contract over time.

For me, the *idea* of tending my garden as a driving and inspirational force is far easier than actually living it. Right now, I am a great juggler with far more deadlines and life responsibilities than I normally experience. Much is being untended, unplanted, unweeded, and unappreciated in my garden now. Nevertheless, it is no less a priority to me. It has just taken a different hierarchical position in the flow and content of my days. No doubt you can completely understand and relate to my position!

I have said a hundred times that I started my garden and motherhood at the same time. I knew nothing about either. Learning how to grow and nurture a garden and two young boys at the same time wasn't easy, but it was *possible*. So, if you are fitting in gardening between office hours, diaper changes, soccer practice, and prescription refills for loved ones, I get it.

So, while I never perfected the art and practice of gardening time management, I did learn a few tricks and strategies that kept things moving forward and never going *completely* off the rails. If you are a new gardener especially, maybe these tips will flatten the learning curve for you of making gardening a priority.

1. Start Small

I can't stress enough the importance of not biting off more than you can chew at the beginning. Dabble first, *then* dive in. Experience the rush of a little success, and then let that motivate you to do more. Do one thing at a time, do it well, learn how, and then move on to the next thing. How you interpret that is up to you; you are the best gauge for what you can and cannot do and how lasting your enthusiasm is for any given project, large or small. It might mean just one or two large pots, or a couple of raised beds (not eight) or a smaller garden bed that you later expand as you move up the learning curve. For me, that meant an original, relatively simple garden design that I had someone else develop and install. I learned how to take care and tend it, then added a lot more complexity and plantings down the line. Even now, I constantly am asking myself the question: Is this too much for what I have going on right now in my life? I also know that if I don't take the time and energy to do it right the first time, it will undoubtedly be harder and more expensive the second time.

Inelegantly put, it is better to have less that is well cared for and mindfully tended and cultivated (with plans for the areas you simply haven't tackled yet) than to have half of your yard torn up and looking, well, half-arsed and sloppy because you spread yourself too thin at the outset.

"A clip-clip here, clip-clip there, and a couple of tra-la-las. . . . That's how we laugh the day away in the merry old land of Oz!" Or in my potager! A little bit of clipping whenever I can sneak off to the potager divides the work and makes the task less burdensome. Especially when cleanup is easy by putting a tarp under the boxwood to catch clippings.

2. Work in the Margins

Even now, as an empty nester with a flexible work schedule and fewer family commitments, I seldom have time to dedicate a full morning or afternoon, much less a whole weekend, to tending the garden. Large blocks of time like that for most of us are few and far between. I no longer put things off, thinking I will tackle this or that chore when I have time for a gardening marathon. *It ain't gonna happen.* That planned marathon is usually rained out, usurped by a quick trip to wherever, or if it's an especially beautiful day consumed by gardening reverie instead of garden toil.

I have learned to work in the margins of my day. If I have an extra hour, I will tackle the back porch and my topiaries. Thirty minutes might mean seeding the basil and pinching back the zinnias. My morning stroll, with coffee and still in my pjs gives me time for both enjoying the garden and assessing what needs to be done that day—that I will sprinkle in here and there as I find five or ten minutes and need to stretch my back and legs from too much computer time. Even a couple of minutes can mean spritzing the tomatoes for spider mite or pulling a few weeds here and there.

3. Make It Convenient to be Efficient

I could have written *several* books over the years in the amount of time I have spent looking for things I needed for this or that garden chore. Though I have much room for growth in this area, I *have* learned that if I can readily get my hands on those pruners, garden gloves, insecticidal sprays, or hand tools, I am much more likely to tackle a job before conditions worsen and get out of control. I keep a covered basket/side table on my covered front porch where I store all such necessities, and I can easily grab them for a quick garden chore. I also keep bug spray and sunscreen at the ready. I also recommend hanging some garden snips on a hook right next to your back door to grab whenever you head out for a quick garden stroll or when the kids are on the swing set. There is always a flower to be deadheaded, sedum to be sheared back, or vine to be contained. And of course, do as I say, not as

In between takes on a video shoot, I pick up my sprayer to target some offending spider mites.

I do. Try to put things back in the same storage area after completion each time. One mistake I made was to create multiple locations for such things, which resulted, of course, in always having to check multiple locations to find something—and that assumes of course that I put it back to begin with. *Note to self:* Find a storage system that works and then work that system! By the way, I am also still working on a workable system for locating my coffee cup, glass of wine, and cell phone. #GARDENGOALS—LOL!

4. Use Technology to Your Advantage

When I first started my garden, there were no plant identifier apps, Google search functions, or helpful online resources. There were books and real people and local horticulture extension centers and garden clubs. And I exploited all of them in my hunger for information. Now, with a few clicks on my handheld device, I can find an organic, homemade treatment for powdery mildew, how to espalier my apple tree, and why I should consider this variety over that for my growing zone. I still rely on those other resources, of course. There is no substitute for visiting with someone in your own neighborhood who has found a solution to a vexing garden issue you too are experiencing.

But I must confess, I get asked so many questions on social media as a supposed expert that I have no educated answer for—but I still want to be

helpful. What should I do? I search reliable websites that I can pass on to the questioner that are based on current existing science and best practices. All at my fingertips. Now, if you asked me a subjective question on design or personal preferences, that's a whole different matter. Those fall in the realm of the largely subjective and I usually have an opinion on the matter. Not necessarily right or wrong, but since you asked . . .

5. Plant Less of More, and More of Less

I heartily endorse trying to grow something new to you each year. It keeps gardening exciting and fresh, grows new neural pathways as we learn new things, and keeps us open to possibilities of untried favorite plants and garden experiences. But as a very wise gardener just reminded me this past weekend, the best advice she could share with a new gardener would be to plant more of whatever works. That is, of course, if you like it and it likes you.

Large, broad swaths of something healthy and beautiful is far more appealing than sad and sorry little blobs of unhappy strugglers. I have found this to be true even in my relatively small garden without sweeping vistas and large expansive flower borders. Plus, I can divide these happy garden residents around the garden and with others, saving both time and money. It is just the kind of simple, practical thing that makes for classic elegance in the garden.

6. Manage Expense

Gardening *can* be an expensive hobby but doesn't *have* to be. Doing your research on the front end about certain plants and design schemes will save you money and heartache down the road. A quart-size plant is less pricey than a two-gallon (8 L) size specimen and will probably establish itself and thrive more readily than its more mature counterpart. Seeds are cheaper than a cell pack of the same plant and have a smaller carbon footprint. Soliciting starts and division from friends is a wise move, with the added benefit of knowing its history of success and provenance. I have traded out many hours of design advice and social media exposure for free plants, tools, and garden maintenance services. I have also cultivated a network of friends in the industry who alert me to special pricing, bargains, or even giveaways of plants I might want or plants I am having difficulty finding. Reciprocity is crucial, of course. I do the same for them whenever I spy something that suits their garden style or color scheme.

Be opportunistic and exploit what is already growing in your own garden. The beautiful redbud canopy that shelters my gravel dining deck was created by nurturing and tending tiny volunteers over time. I then pruned them as they grew and gave them extra TLC so they would mature and flourish. I have propagated many cuttings from my own herbs, shrubs, and annuals, simply by rooting them in water and planting them elsewhere in the gardenscape. If I am trying to fill a void in one garden bed or container, I always shop my own garden first. If there is a candidate that is not flourishing where it currently exists and might be much happier in the new location I have in mind, then it is fodder for my shovel. I recently dug up two hostas that were very average in one congested bed—and replanted them in an empty window box where they are now considerably happier and thriving. Win-wins are everywhere in your landscape. And you won't even need to get in the car.

When my liriope gets too thick and needs thinning, or when my rudbeckia self-seeds too much even for me, I let others know that if they come and get it, it's theirs. My labor is saved, and they get free plants.

Finally, patience and delayed gratification will save you untold pennies, prevent expensive mistakes, and will probably be better for the health and vitality of your garden in the long run. As for character building and self-growth, I am told it helps in that regard as well, but personally I have little to show for it.

Six Gardening Superpowers

Work on developing these six superpowers to become a more effective, healthy, and successful gardener.

1. **Consistency:** The most important superpower of all. Whether its watering, feeding, deadheading, or harvesting, being consistent and reliable about your garden tasks will reward you beyond measure.
2. **Curiosity:** Fostering curiosity about both the good and bad things you observe in your garden will prevent problems and enhance the garden experience for you. It is the foundation for continued learning.
3. **Capacity for delight:** Truly, the key to the fountain of youth and maybe to happiness itself.
4. **Common sense:** Practice common sense when it comes to your own safety, what is unhealthy for the environment, and what is good for your family and community.
5. **Context:** Don't fight Mother Nature, your neighbors, or your own limitations. Always consider your garden in context.
6. **Community:** A garden is a gift. Share it.

Joy can be found in the garden in every season. Each season, no matter where you live, has its own special gifts, rewards, and traditions. Growing a garden enriches and enhances these differences in a way nothing else can.

I am the attending physician of my own garden. I make daily rounds to ensure the health and vigor of my garden, and the mental and physical health of myself, as the garden's caregiver.

"GARDENERS, LIKE EVERYONE ELSE, LIVE SECOND BY SECOND
AND MINUTE BY MINUTE. WHAT WE SEE AT ONE PARTICULAR MOMENT IS
THEN AND THERE BEFORE US. BUT THERE IS A SECOND WAY OF SEEING. SEEING
WITH THE EYE OF MEMORY, NOT THE EYE OF OUR ANATOMY,
CALLS UP DAYS AND SEASONS PAST AND YEARS GONE BY."
—ALLEN LACY, *THE GARDENER'S EYE*

Chapter 9

COMMUNITY AND SEASONAL CELEBRATION

HARVEST JOY AND LIVE A GARDEN LIFE

When I started my gardens years ago, I did it selfishly. I wanted to be surrounded by a garden's beauty and partake of its garden gifts: to have a creative pastime, abundant flowers and vegetables for my home, and an idyllic backdrop to start my new family. I was motivated by envy. I wanted a landscape and surroundings rivalling those of some of my neighbors and friends and the incredible images I saw in my treasured garden books.

In other words, gardening was all about me and my family, and what I could get out of it. It wasn't until I had gardened for a while that I realized what a joyous *gift* a garden could be—not just to me, but to my neighborhood, my community, and even my city. I realized what power a garden could really engender once I started sharing it more with others, in both practical *hands-on* and *how-to* ways through garden tours, fundraisers, and workshops, but also in personal, heartfelt, people-connecting communal ways. Let me relate a few of my own experiences where the garden was savored in ways I could have never orchestrated intentionally. These encounters happened organically, by virtue of just growing a front yard garden that attracted people and conversation to it.

Huge coral pink azaleas (*Rhododendron*), tufted pine cones, olive tree foliage, contorted branches, and fern fronds from the garden make for a nontraditional fall table centerpiece—reason enough to gather together, share a seasonal meal, and make others feel important.

The Easter Parade Family Portrait: On a particularly beautiful Saturday morning, the Saturday before Easter, a young man drove up to my front curb in a pickup truck with tinted windows. He asked if he could take a picture of the hundreds of tulips then in bloom. I said, "Of course," and stepped out of the frame only to see that there was a sweet little girl in a car seat in the back, holding an Easter basket in her tiny lap, filled with goodies from the Easter egg hunt she had just attended. I asked the young man if he would like his daughter to be in the picture with her Easter basket—that it would make such a fun Easter image. He was thrilled with the idea and asked if his wife could be in it too. She was sitting in the passenger seat but was hidden from my view because of the darkened glass. I laughed and said, "Of course!" and offered to take picture of the three of them. After many takes and multiple poses and lots of bunny frivolity, they thanked me profusely and got back into their truck. But the mother lingered a bit, took me aside, and earnestly thanked me again. It was, she told me appreciatively, *very* special—it was their first family picture since her husband had returned home safely from Iraq. Special? I do believe so. To both of us.

In the spring, hundreds of sorbet-colored tulips *(Tulipa)* turn my front yard into a living Easter egg—a perfect backdrop for Easter pictures of littles with their bunnies and baskets. Ferny, fine-leaved chamomile looks and smells delicate and sweet, dancing with the large headed tulips.

An Elderly Neighbor: My old urban neighborhood is a friendly one and notices about upcoming parades, holiday lightings, and litter cleanups in our park are often tucked in our door. On one occasion, I had a card, written in a very shaky hand. It was from one of my older neighbors, a woman I had never met who wrote me a thank you note. I have it still—a treasured item I keep tucked in a favorite gardening book. She says, "I just want to thank you for all of the joy your garden has brought me over the years. I know how hard you work on it. I am too old to garden, and so I would 'borrow' yours. It gave me special happiness whenever I would go by. I never stopped to tell you because I didn't want to disturb or bother you. But now I am moving into a nursing home, and I wanted to thank you and let you know I will still be taking your garden with me. I have lots of pictures I have taken of it over the years, and I will have them to enjoy even when I am far from home. They will keep me from feeling so homesick. Here are some copies of them for you. Your neighbor, Edna."

The Lady in High Heels: Spring comes early to my Oklahoma front garden, which faces south. Tulips and phlox, azaleas and cabbages, lettuces and lacy chamomile put on their show starting in late March, continuing into the first two weeks of April. At the end of my block is a rather large church, and on this particular April weekend, it was holding a wedding. As I stood up to stretch from my garden work, I could see a woman in teetery high heels, all dressed up, bustling her way toward me, traveling the length of the block from the church parking lot to catch me in the garden. She said she had never seen anything like it. It had completely changed her ideas about Oklahoma, she exclaimed. She was from Maine and had no idea we could grow such things so beautifully this far south and so early in the season. It was her first visit to our state and as spring was still so far away in her Maine garden that she asked to take lots of pictures and notes so she could replicate some ideas in her own garden before her spring arrived. "What a pleasant, pleasant surprise!" she clucked nicely, never expecting to find such a sight on her trip. Then in a flash, as quickly as she had arrived, she clicked her heels, thanked me for the spring show, and bustled back down the street in her Sunday best and high heels for the rest of the wedding reception. Who knew? I was just glad she hadn't visited in the dead of the summer! The story would have a much different ending.

Front Yard Garden Etiquette

If I were queen of the world or at least my neighborhood, I would institute these rules for etiquette and comportment when approaching someone working in their garden. On most occasions, gardeners are happy to oblige and like nothing better than to talk of gardens and gardening. But there are exceptions that most of us can relate to.

Rule 1: Do NOT stop to make small talk, ask questions with lengthy answers, or in any way keep the gardener occupied in conversation if they are in their pajamas or are scantily clad but still couldn't resist pulling that weed, looking at that flower, or squishing that snail en route to getting the paper, taking out the trash, or just quickly moving the car into the drive. One would think this obvious, but most gardeners will say this is not always the case. It also applies to anyone with curlers in their hair, a face mask on, or who are wiggling like they may have to use the potty.

Rule 2: Do NOT pepper the gardener with lots of questions as to "if what you have growing in your garden will work in theirs" until after you have gushed profusely about what is growing then and there in said gardener's garden.

Rule 3: Gardeners who spend a lot of time, money, and sweat equity on their front landscapes are suckers for a compliment. As you stroll by an exceptionally beautiful garden and catch the eye of the gardener, don't pretend you didn't notice how extraordinary it is. Say something to acknowledge the beauty and hard work involved.

Rule 4: And as for me, I am generally happy to show you my garden at any time of year, even if it is not at its best. Except late summer. Please, not in late summer. It's simply too hot and I don't even want to be out there to see the garden sweltering in the late summer heat. Trust me on this one.

I love the overlap of the seasons when fresh lettuces and parsley enjoy the same temperatures cold enough to warrant a cozy fire after harvesting them. A silver-plated bowl with spring greens is every bit as beautiful in its own way as a large bouquet of flowers and makes an unexpected seasonal centerpiece.

Of course, for each story I shared, there are countless others, and I bet you have many of your own equally as poignant—how your garden delighted someone passing by, inspired them, or simply gave them a pleasant break from a difficult day. Since I live in the heart of the city, I may have more than most, and I'm often asked if it bothers me to be interrupted so frequently by people with questions or picture-takers or to exchange pleasantries and conversation whether I know them or not. So here is my last story to tell. A very personal one, and one that informs my thoughts on sharing my garden with others.

Several or more years ago, when my elderly father was telling stories at a family reunion with most of his ten children and some grandchildren listening in, he responded to some questions we asked him about the months and days after our first mother died. She was just thirty-six and left my father with seven young children from age one to twelve. It was a topic we seldom broached and knew little about. She died on a beautiful Saturday in May, and over the course of the following weeks, he related that he would put my baby sister in the stroller walking alongside my younger brother and me. I was five at the time. He said we would pepper him with questions like, "How would she get a drink of water?" or, "How will she know how to find us?" We were, he said pensively, a very motley, sad crew walking down the street. He also said that on a number of those evenings he would see neighbors working in their front yards who would see us coming their way. Looking into the distance thoughtfully, he then commented that when they saw our pitiful group approaching, they often went inside. "It was," he guessed out loud, "just too sad for them and they didn't know what to say. But it would have been nice to visit with them for a while. It would have been nice," he said.

So, if someone is walking down the street and heading my way, and they seem to want to stop and chat for a minute, I try to remember that. A garden, along with a bit of your time and a caring ear, can be a very large and important gift indeed.

A hanging basket filled with the essence of fall: gourds, berries, and greens.

"SUMMER AFTERNOON, SUMMER AFTERNOON; TO ME THOSE HAVE ALWAYS BEEN THE
TWO MOST BEAUTIFUL WORDS IN THE ENGLISH LANGUAGE."
—HENRY JAMES

THROUGH THE SEASONS

Well, I hate to quibble with the great Henry James, but I most adamantly disagree. Most of us in our steamy, brutally hot summer gardens would beg to differ, typically preferring the milder months in spring and fall. Instead, I would say "Gardening through the seasons" would be my nominee for the award. I guess whether or not you agree with him depends on where you live and what outdoor conditions you prefer. Gardeners are individualistic that way. I like that about us.

Whichever your favorite season or sub season— for I have found every season has its sub seasons within it—celebrate it with inspiration, materials, colors, and produce from the garden. Engage and encourage others to join in. For I do agree with this famous quote *"I shall pass this way but once; any good that I can do or any kindness I can show to any human being; let me do it now. Let me not defer nor neglect it, for I shall not pass this way again."* Each season of each year is a thing unique, individualistic in its time just like the gardener. This specific season, in this specific year, at this specific time will not visit us again. So why not savor it? Even in the harshest of seasons, there are endowments from our gardens. Even if we only harvest a lesson learned, a battle overcome, or permission to concede what we can no longer nurture.

The change in seasons is a perfect time to celebrate. These seasonal transitions are usually accompanied by a noticeable and exquisite change in the quality of light—golden and low, high and searing, or long or short in shadows, and of course the length of the daylight itself. The characteristics of changing light alone are reason enough to celebrate, along with seasonal fresh fruits and vegetables, cooler or warmer temperatures, and more or less annoying/pleasant bugs and flying wildlife. In other words, always look for ways to exploit what each season brings. One thing I have learned as I've gotten older and gardened longer, is that such festivities and marks of time and seasons passing must be *intentional*. Which to me means a bit of planning is required. Even if it's nothing more than checking the seven-day forecast or knowing which weekends are typically the busiest for others and might be a conflict. (Think summer weddings, graduations, football games, office holiday parties. You get the point.) Happily, these seasonal fetes need not be elaborate or grand. Simply elegant in their simplicity and their focus on the gifts of that season.

Gracious living day to day, season to season, generation to generation.

Fruits of the Season

Is there anything better than a fresh picked peach or cherry straight from the tree?

Nothing speaks to the season of spring and summer like fruit trees. Both ornamental and practical, their beautiful blossoms transform to edible fruit as the seasons change. Fruit trees in general prefer well-drained soil and a sunny location. Most varieties take time to start producing fruit, but they are well worth the wait as the trees mature and get established. The varieties below were recommended and selected for the widest range of growing zones. In my next garden—whether a small espalier or a large orchard—I am going to have my own fruit trees from which to pluck. What dreams are made of. I may start with one or two of these recommendations from the Arbor Day Foundation.

PLUM
- Recommended variety 'Purple Leaf' *Prunus cerasifera*
- Grows 15–25 feet (5–8 m) tall by 15–20 feet (5–6 m) wide
- Low maintenance and adaptable
- Need two to bear fruit (three years before producing fruit)
- Dwarf variety suggestion: 'Santa Rosa' *Prunus salacina* (*Prunus salacina* 'Santa Rosa')
- No reliable dwarf rootstock for plums, may have to prune

PEACH
- Recommended variety: 'Reliance' *Prunus persica*
- Grows 9–15 feet (3–5 m) tall by 12–15 feet (4–5 m) wide
- Easy to grow with abundant harvests
- Most are self-pollinating (two years before producing fruit)
- Dwarf variety suggestion: 'Bonfire' patio peach (*Prunus persica* 'Bonfire')

PEAR
- Recommended variety: 'Anjou' *Pyrus communis*
- Grows 12–18 feet (4–6 m) tall by 8–20 feet (2–6 m) wide
- Pears can be enjoyed fresh or used in savory and sweet recipes
- Most varieties will need two years to bear fruit (three years before producing fruit)
- Dwarf variety suggestion: 'Dwarf Bartlett' pear (*Pyrus communis* 'Bartlett')

CHERRY
- Recommended variety: 'Montmorency' *Prunus cerasus*
- Grows 8–18 feet (2–6 m) tall by 10–20 feet (3–6 m) wide
- Sweet cherries best for raw eating
- Need two to three trees for pollination (four years until it produces fruit)
- Dwarf variety suggestion: Juliet™ dwarf cherry (*Prunus fruticosa* x *Prunus cerasus* 'Big Red')

Spring: Why Not Try To. . .

- Tiptoe through the tulips and have a tea party.
- Cut stems of forsythia, quince, apple, or pear trees to force and bring inside to hasten spring blooms.
- Fill a large platter or urn with all spring green veggies: cabbage, celery, pea pods, and asparagus and then put a skirt of cilantro and parsley around the edges. Use as a verdant, dramatic centerpiece. Extra credit for arranging it on a yellow, pink, or lavender platter.
- Plant a living Easter basket with a bed of microgreens, baby lettuces, or rye grass. Just add jellybeans and a chocolate bunny for a basket to remember.
- Let someone else do the work. Buy pre-forced hyacinths, daffodils, and tulips from your grocer, florist, or garden center. Then plant in a beautiful container. Then add your own pots of pansies, snapdragons, and violas to create a quick and easy container planting display for your front porch or terrace.
- Invite your child's first grade class to come make Tussie Mussies from your garden for Mother's Day, or May Day baskets to surprise and delight a neighbor.

Spring onions about to burst into bloom.

Make your own garden photo gallery wall by selecting images from your own garden that you find beautiful. Classic blooms are pretty but look for the more unusual stages of a plant's circle of life to inspire you. Consider where you will place them, what colors you want to emphasize, and how you can best show them off. Have fun with the framing process. You may find that some types of plants lend themselves more to one room over another: veggies for the kitchen, herbs for the bath, bare winter branches for the library. It's an easy way to bring the garden indoors and inexpensively decorate your home in the process.

Spring Project: Framed Images from Your Garden

What you'll need:
- Images of herbal seed and flower heads Frames (I used 4, but you could have more framed images for your wall grid)

I am in the process of redoing some interior spaces and of course, I wanted to bring the garden inside in some way. I love the look of herbal blooms and seed heads, especially when beautifully photographed. These ethereal images of dill, parsley, allium, and mint make a perfect visual anthology for a gallery wall. As you can see, there is room to add to the collection over time.

Summer : Why Not Try To. . .

- Host a pesto making party to use up all that basil before it goes to seed. Or maybe use spinach, kale, chard, or cilantro. Whatever you have in abundance in your garden.
- Hold a garden tour fundraiser for your favorite charity when the weather is at its most welcoming and the potager its most bountiful.
- Host a wedding shower when the hydrangeas are at their peak. Pre-cut some bouquets for the bride's mother, grandmother, or sisters to take home with them.
- Host a weeding party out in the vegetable garden. Set up a picnic in the cool of the evening with baguettes, delicious spreads, mustards, and condiments. Prepare platters of grilled vegetables, grilled and fresh fruits, and have lots of ice-chilled beverages for the kids and adults. You can host a weeding party in any season because every season is weed season!
- Paint an old piece of furniture the same color as your 'Ichiban' eggplant or your orange habanero peppers.
- Host a coffee, tea, and pastries party in the potager just after dawn and before the heat sets in. Maybe Breakfast at Wimbledon? Invite guests to bring baskets to take home garden-fresh vegetables—just enough for dinner that night. A random act of dinner kindness at its freshest!

Above: Grow your own cocktail garden! This planter was inspired by a pineapple-mint mojito recipe courtesy of the National Wildlife Federation. Recipe on facing page.

Left: Gold spray-painted dried leek (*Allium ampeloprasum*) and allium seed heads make festive sparklers for summer celebrations in any country or language. Freshly cut hydrangea blooms, spike speedwell (*Veronica spicata*) spires and red gerbera daisies (*Gerbera jamesonii*) complete the arrangement.

Refreshing Mojito

Why not try making this refreshing pineapple-mint mojito with fresh mint from your own garden. Your garden guests, pollinators, and humans alike will thank you for it.

MINT

ICE

WHITE RUM

LIME

CLUB SODA

1. Muddle mint leaves and add to a tall glass.

2. Muddle the lime and add the juice to the glass.

3. Add the sugar to the glass and crush slightly with a pestle.

4. Add a few drops of hot water to dissolve the sugar. Let stand for 2–3 minutes.

5. Pour the rum and cold pineapple juice into the glass and stir.

6. Add ice and top off with soda.

Recipe card for pineapple-mint mojito, compliments of the National Wildlife Federation.

Summer Project: Plant a Pollinator Mojito Garden

What you'll need (depending on the scale of your mojito garden):

- 4" (10 cm) mint (multiples if desired)
- Lavender/basil/pineapple sage for pollinator interest
- All-purpose potting soil
- Container of choice

Anyone can grow the ingredients needed for this summer fresh pineapple-mint mojito—the mint anyway! Pineapples are in short supply growing in my garden. The recipe is courtesy of the National Wildlife Federation, which held a campaign to encourage us gardeners to plant for pollinating wildlife. A long, cool drink on a hot summer day was all the encouragement I needed. Play with the ingredients in your own herb garden to concoct cocktails or mocktails unique to your own garden and lifestyle, then own it proudly!

This intoxicating cocktail engages all the senses in the very best way. Leave out rum for a mocktail version.

Fall: Why Not Try To . . .

- Hold an apple-tasting party in the fall. Set it up in the potager and ask everyone to bring a different variety of apples.
- Get a small fire grate and kindling to set up wherever and whenever—for picnicking, camping, or on your driveway for the first marshmallows and roasted hot dogs of the season.
- Cut and dry garden herbs to give as holiday gifts later in the year.
- Plant tiny tete-a-tete daffodil bulbs as a sweet border to your lettuce greens, parsley, or cilantro to enjoy next spring.
- Use small pumpkins and gourds to mulch and adorn your large pots and container gardens. Tuck them into window boxes, prop them in metal tuteurs, line them up on your outdoor kitchen window, and then plan on chasing the squirrels away!
- Use hollow stems of tall, dried alliums like 'Globemaster' or 'Ambassador' and use them to support and lengthen floppy or short-stemmed blooms in flower arrangements. Or use them to showcase dried hydrangea blooms, interesting seed heads, or other dried garden confections.

Above: A simple wooden bowl with freshly picked apples, cut sections of Encore® azaleas whose branches mimic the look of apple branches, and a string of fairy lights creates a delightful still life.

Left: For a more dramatic display, arrange a statement-making bouquet by adding pokeweed berries, gray seeded eucalyptus, and more apples and and Autumn Bonfire® Encore azaleas. Actually, almost any cuttings from the shrubs in your own garden will do nicely in your arrangement.

Fall Project: Hanging Basket of Autumn

What you'll need (depending on the size of your basket):

- Hanging basket with liner, no smaller than 16" (40 cm) in diameter; preferably larger
- One to three 4" (10 cm) 'Winterbor' kale (or kale of choice)
- 1 gallon (4 L) 'Buttered Rum' heucherella (reduce root ball)
- 1 gallon (4 L) Flirt™ nandina (reduce root ball)
- Lightweight potting mix
- Nandina berries
- Small pumpkins or gourds
- Clear gloss acrylic spray

Place a round of burlap or tulle under coir liner to deter squirrels and birds from pecking at fiber. Fill the basket with a lightweight potting mix. Gently tease roots from nandina and heucherella and reduce root ball size. Loosen root balls of kale. Plant to taste, filling in gaps with more soil. Hang, then water well. Tuck in gourds, pumpkins, and berries to perfection.

A fall project: creating a hanging basket of 'Winterbor' kale, 'Buttered Rum' heucherella, Flirt™ nandina, and tiny pumpkins, with nandina berries tucked in.

Winter Project: Bark Vase for Holiday Display

What you'll need:
- Large can or container of choice. I used a Folgers coffee container.
- Glue gun
- Detached bark of any kind from firewood, woods, etc.
- Extra moss and lichens for seams
- Rubber bands
- Chicken wire for stem support
- Garden fresh greenery, flowers, herbs, or live plants of your choice. Pine cones for a decorative, seasonal flourish.

Gather supplies. Forage wood from your own woodpile or a forest floor from which you have permission to scavenge. Wash and dry container of choice. Glue sections of bark with a hot glue gun, trim off the bottom pieces to be flush with the bottom of the container. Do the same on the top rim, unless you want some of the sections to be taller and irregular. Put several large rubber bands around the circumference of the container to ensure bark-to-container contact while it dries. Fill in any gaps with moss, bits of lichen, or other woodsy material. Adorn with pine cones if desired. Use as a vase or a planter as desired with chicken wire to secure stems (optional). Let the season determine the theme for what you showcase in your rustic vase.

With little to no expense, and just a bit of your time, you can create a seasonal masterpiece.

Winter: Why Not Try To . . .

- Dry some of your 'Cowhorn' okra pods from last summer, spray painting them your holiday color of choice, and hanging them as Christmas ornaments. You can use acorns, fall gourds, and pine cones too.
- Cut dried hydrangea blooms and spray paint them—or leave them natural—to use as flocking on your tree or to adorn packages. Just tuck them in between branches or in ribboned boxes.
- Harvest rosemary to make toasted rosemary-honey almonds for holiday gifting. Search for any number of recipes online.
- Make a tower of citrus with stacked cake plates. Tuck in cuttings of rosemary, bay, and lemon leaves for a fragrant holiday centerpiece. Extra credit for clove-studded citrus, sugared fruit (use an egg wash and superfine sugar) and mixing your citrus—kumquats, oranges, clementines, and grapefruit. For the kids, poke citrus-flavored candy sticks in the tufts of herbs.
- Create your own personalized seed packets with a custom-made emblem for your garden. Fill them with seeds from your gardens and use as stocking stuffers.

The garden and its seasons give, and we partake. It is an exchange. We give to our gardens, and they give back. Not always in equal measure, but still—with great passion, optimism, and learning. Gardening, I have discovered, is not just a hobby, a pastime, or even a way to make a living.

For me, it is a calling. An elegant calling.

I hope you too will experience the joy, humility, and gratitude of answering its call.

PRODUCTS AND RESOURCES

GENERAL

Linda Vater—For the Home on QVC.com
Practical and beautiful home and garden accessories for garden-inspired living.

Gardeners.com

"Ergonomic Tools That Can Ease Gardening Pains" by Jim Miller, the Savvy Senior
Ergonomic tools to protect your back, hands, knees, and more.

GLOVES

Pine Tree Tools Bamboo Working Gloves, made from soft breathable bamboo that absorbs moisture to keep your hands cool in the summer and warm in the winter. The palms and fingers are coated with nitrile, which is a thin and flexible synthetic rubber that provides excellent grip and can withstand punctures and even small thorns. These gloves are even touchscreen friendly so you can make reminders on your smart phone or tablet without taking your gloves off. Available in five sizes. PineTreeTools.com.

DIGGING AND WEEDING

Radius Garden Ergonomic Hand Tools have a large, curved handle that's easier to grip and keeps your wrist in a natural straight position to reduce injury. Individual ergonomic tools include the trowel, transplanter, weeder, and cultivator. RadiusGarden.com.

CobraHead Long Handle Weeder and Cultivator is a steel hook-shaped blade that flares at the tip, resembling the head of a cobra that requires you to primarily use your arm muscles to dig and chop into the soil from a standing position. CobraHead.com.

Fiskars Stand-Up Weed Puller makes it easy to remove invasive plants without kneeling down or bending over. Just place the head over a weed, step down on the foot platform, and the four serrated, stainless-steel claws will grab the weed by the root for clean removal. Fiskers.com.

Root Slayer is a multi-purpose shovel/hatchet/saw that makes digging and planting much easier. It comes with an O-shaped handle that allows you to comfortably grip it with both hands for better leverage. RadiusGarden.com.

BackEZ is an ergonomically designed auxiliary handle that can be added to any long-handled gardening tool (shovel, hoe, pitchfork, or rake) to help you work more comfortably with less strain on your back and shoulders. BackEZ.net.

KNEE AND BACKSAVER

TomCare UpGraded Garden Kneeler Seat is a multipurpose kneepad with steel support handles to help you raise and lower yourself. Or flip it over and it becomes a padded bench to sit on for weeding or planting. Lightweight and foldable, it also comes with two pouches to hold your tools when you're working. Amazon.com.

PRUNING

Felco 7 Revolving Handle Pruning Shears comes with an ergonomic handle that rotates when you squeeze it to reduce hand and wrist strain. It's sharp, smooth, and very durable, and requires minimal hand strength to cut even the thickest of branches. Felco.com.

WATERING

TheFitLife Flexible and Expandable Garden Hose is incredibly lightweight, easy to move around and store. It expands to three times it's extension length and weighs between 2 and 4.5 pounds (1 and 2 kg) depending on the length you choose—25, 50, 75 or 100 feet (or 8, 15, 23 or 30 m). TheFitLifeStore.com.

Gardenite 10-Pattern Garden Hose Nozzle is a versatile, heavy duty spray nozzle that has a soft ergonomic hand grip and trigger lock so you can water for long periods without hand fatigue. Gardenite.com.

SeCa Hose Holder provides a convenient hands-free use of the water hose for watering and cleaning up and eliminates bending over to pick up the hose. SeCaHoseHolder.com.

SEED AND BULB SOURCES

Annie's Annuals & Perennials

anniesannuals.com

Specializes in rare and unusual plants

Breck's Bulbs

brecks.com

Perennials and flower bulbs

Colorblends Bulbs

colorblends.com

Specializes in bulb blends of all kinds

John Scheepers Kitchen Garden Seeds

kitchengardenseeds.com

Family-owned and operated, sells seeds for fruits, vegetables, flowers, and herbs

Johnny's Selected Seeds

johnnyseeds.com

Sells seeds for fruits, vegetables, flowers, and herbs; offers certified organic seed options

Pinetree Garden Seeds

superseeds.com

Wide variety of vegetable and flower seeds at economical prices

Prairie Moon Nursery

prairiemoon.com

Plants, seed mixes, and information for all types of native plantings and restoration

Renee's Garden Seeds

reneesgarden.com

Seeds for gourmet vegetables, herbs, and cut flowers, especially large sweet pea flower collection

Seed Savers Exchange

seedsavers.org

Heirloom and old-fashioned seeds; committed to preserving biodiversity

Territorial Seed Company

territorialseed.com

Specializes in wide variety of vegetable seeds

ACKNOWLEDGMENTS

The Elegant and Edible Garden would not have been possible without the constant encouragement from my followers to *"Please write a book,"* my photographer Stewart Perryman and helpful LV team members, and the patience and support of the three men in my life, my "hubs" Jamie and my sons Johnny and Jamie, and my nine brothers and sisters.

I'd also like to thank my friend, DD, who kept telling me *"You can do hard things"* when there just seemed no way to accomplish all that needed to be done.

Mostly, I want to thank the garden itself, for being my muse, my protector, and my salvation.

ABOUT THE AUTHOR

Linda Vater is a self-taught garden designer, stylist, writer, and media producer who obsesses over garden-inspired living indoors and out. She represents the Linda Vater brand through her website lindavater.com and through her social media platforms, on a TV segment on NBC local affiliate KFOR, through her product line on QVC, as a contributor to numerous magazines and public speaking, and as a spokesperson for the Southern Living Plant Collection. She has been on more garden tours than she can count and is a firm believer that gardening brings us together. Her mission is to make garden style accessible, affordable, practical, and reassuring.

PHOTO CREDITS

INDEX